D1034539

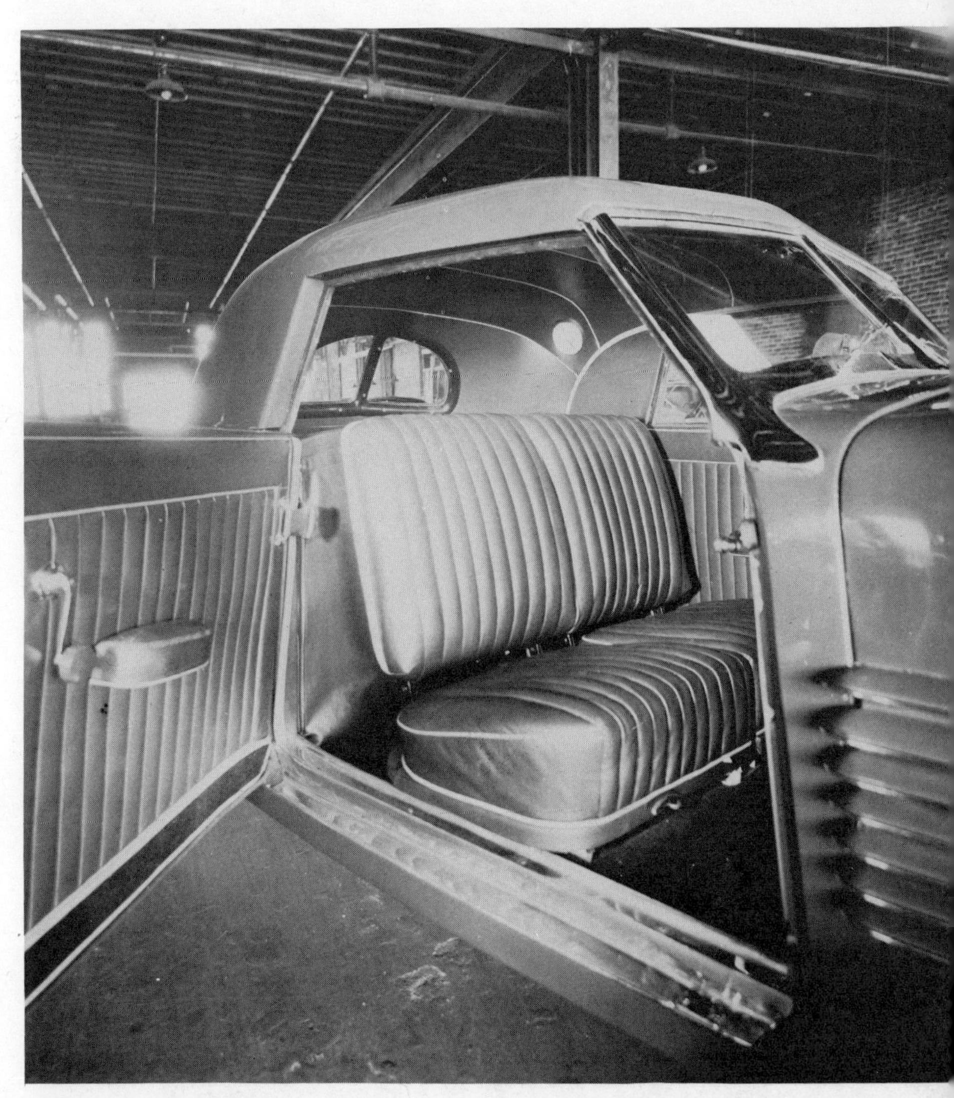

CENTRAL / Cord 810 / WCK

BRUNN / Lincoln / WEM

Essentials of UPHOLSTERY & TRIM for VINTAGE & CLASSIC

with a gallery of interiors from the opulent era

Selected and edited by

Lee Jordan Locke

Post Motor Books
1970
Arcadia CA 91006

Foreword

In those beaming, verdant days when custom bodies were an everyday prerogative of the Titans, and degrees of automotive elegance were limited only by the imagination, this plainly written text was a popular handbook among apprentice trimmers.

Procedure for French plaiting, diamond and bisquit tufting, negligee and plain work, headlining, fabric top construction, *et al*, were covered in everyday language. Supporting layout diagrams left no detail to conjecture.

Today, more than two generations later, the manual is reissued in an expanded, post-era edition to provide the special interest car restorer, as well as, the vocation-minded novice of the Now Generation, with the complete fundamentals of vintage and classic upholstery and trim.

Motoring's golden age of drawing rooms built for the avenue is depicted in many facets through a lavish collection of photographs, selected specially to lend intimate dimension to the considerable latitude custom coachbuilders exercised in pleasing demands of the very rich—from conservative clients to sometimes notably colorful patrons.

The Four Hundred were appeased with trim fabric options from broadlace to velvet and from silk to tapestry. Natural leathers ranged from cowhide to ostrich—and beyond . . .

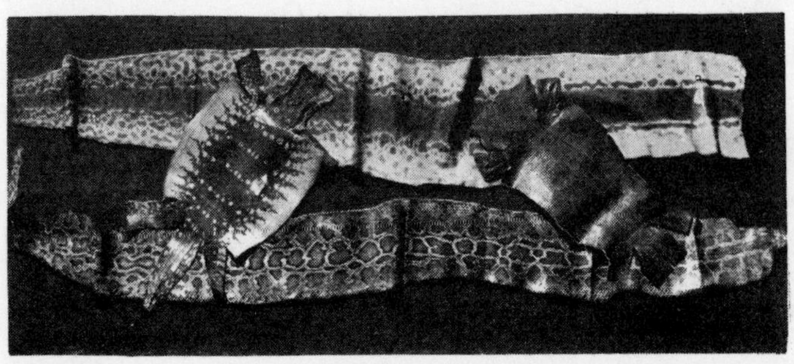

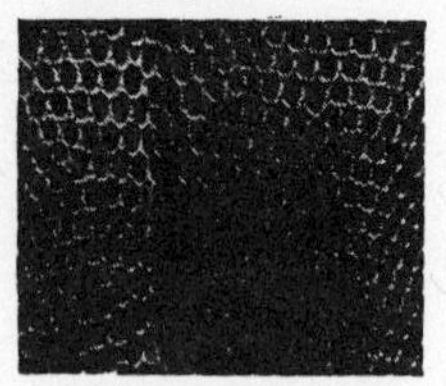

LIZARD

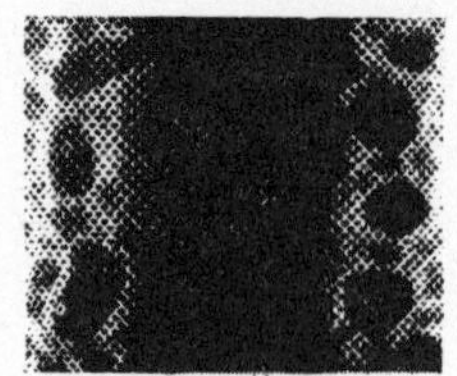

WATERSNAKE

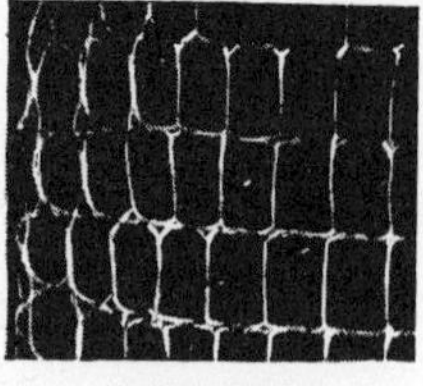

ALLIGATOR

Exotic and beautifully marked skins of snakes, lizards and other reptiles had eluded every effort to preserve them by tanning, until, in the early 'twenties, after extensive French experiments the skins were first successfully processed for commercial use. Results were so satisfactory that reptile hides, tanned in a special plant set up in Berne, Switzerland, finally offered the same durability as those of leathers from fur and wool-bearing animals and fowl. Alligator and lizard accessories for women then began what would become a permanent vogue.

The international set on the French Riviera, and the *avant garde* of Newport society discovered it was suddenly possible to elect automotive interiors using the skins of water snakes, gigantic pythons and boas and deadly cobras from India. And some of them did.

Mobile art works of leading domestic coachbuilders such as the latter day Bohman & Schwartz, the venerable Brewster & Co., Brunn & Co., Derham, Judkins, LeBaron, Locke & Co., Walter M. Murphy Co., Rollston (as well as the outgrowth Rollson), Walker-LeGrande, Waterhouse, Weymann and Willoughby are on exhibit in this showcase of interiors photographs, along with favorites from abroad including coachwork from Castagna, Million-Guiet, H. J. Mulliner, Park Ward and Saoutchik.

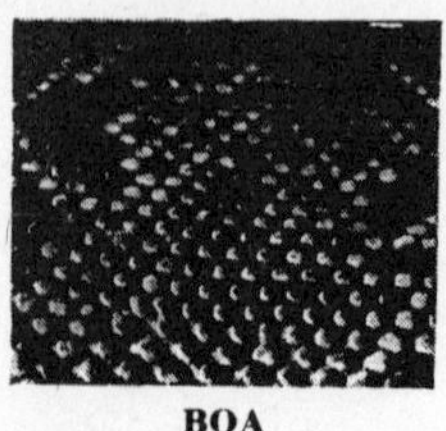

BOA

COBRA

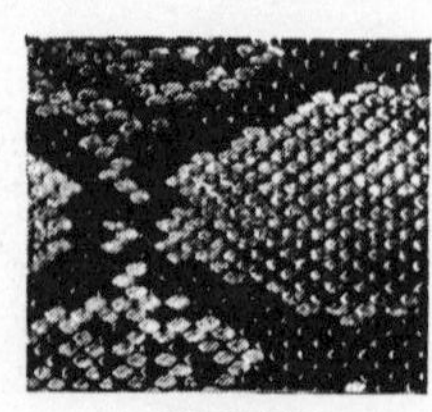

PYTHON

From the days of the horseless carriage—and in the aftermarket—motor trim has remained unchallenged as the cleanest, most orderly and quietest facet in the automotive service field. Seeking a trade associated with his first line of affection, the car-crazy young man of today may confidently choose automobile trimming as a vocation with a rosy future. The capable craftsman is always welcome in this pleasant, satisfying and well-paying profession.

Beginning on the next page the language of this book has been preserved in its original form. The text was slanted for the beginning professional trimmer, taking his apprenticeship in the golden era through a study of the book concurrent with service in a trim shop. It was the motor age of greatest individuality in all automotive specifications. The trimmer's imagination played a distinct role in superior design, layout and detailing. The reader is encouraged to apply his own imagination at every stage.

Chronologically, the text looks back over its shoulder to the elegant trim of the early days and raises its forward sights to cover the simple good taste of the contemporary trim then becoming geared to the mass-market closed car, as well as the overpowering opulence of classic caliber.

Studied today, whether by the restorer as an avocation, or by the uncommitted novice as a lead into the field of motor trim as a career, this book should prove an unfailing friend.

BRUNN / Lincoln / WEM

Contents

Introduction

It should be impressed upon the reader of this book that the purpose of these chapters is to cover that which a thorough mechanic should know about the trimming or upholstering of modern automobiles.

In years gone by a young man served an apprenticeship covering a number of years, during which time he was taught his trade thoroughly and in all its branches.

Today, however, apprenticeships for a trade are not common—each operator becomes a cog in the wheel, so to speak. He is taught but one part of the trade, in other words he specializes, and is given little opportunity for learning the trade in its entirety.

By diligent study and close application, however, the student with the aid of these articles will be assisted wonderfully and become more familiar with the technical and artistic requirements of the all-round trimmer.

And it is well to remember that only those with all round knowledge of the business are considered when there is a vacancy for a trim shop foreman or superintendent.

Vehicle trimming is thoroughly different from any other trade or vocation. It is indeed a valuable art when learned, but very hard to teach, for the reason that it is almost impossible to say where to start. It is unlike other trades inasmuch as there are no set rules or formulas to be followed—no direct lines of application.

The knowledge has been gained altogether at the bench in the shop, and the "rule of thumb" has held sway. For

MURPHY / Duesenberg "Beverly" / CWM

that reason there have been so many ways of accomplishing the same results.

A shop under the supervision of one man has been accustomed to do certain things one way and in another shop an entirely different method is followed.

It seems to be a trade which has been "handed down" from one generation to another, and the characteristics of the man in charge of the shop are often his by right of inheritance.

However, the laying out of automobile upholstery fundamentally rests upon the individual. Rules of proportion, beauty of design, comfort and adaptability to the particular job are the basis on which a trimmer has to work. The trimmer's own experience and the experience of others from whom he takes advice, are his chief guides.

As they are presented, we shall try to make the various problems as clear and distinct as is possible, but the reader must remember that this work is only a text book for the proper studying of methods, and that the student will be called upon to use his own brain in adapting these methods to the work in hand.

To be a successful designer and trimmer one must be the possessor of a creative imagination. When he stands before a new job getting his instructions, his mind must be working and presenting to him a mental picture of the completed job. In no other way can a trimmer become successful as a designer. And this ability is brought about only by hard study and work. Neatness, comfort and durability are essentials of all trimming and upholstery work, and it is experience alone that teaches how to obtain these qualities in your performances.

Duesenberg / CWM

CHAPTER I

The Young Man's Choice of an Occupation

For any young man starting to work, his most serious thought should be upon the question of his future. He should, just as soon as possible, determine for himself what line of work he desires to follow. Having decided what that work is, he must bend every effort to become thoroughly proficient.

The learning of any trade is not solely a question of putting in so many hours each day for a certain period. In addition, it means the hard study of text books, and close observation, not only of what takes place in the shop in which he may be employed, but of the products of his trade, emanating from other establishments, wherever and whenever the opportunity presents itself.

As Sir Joshua Reynolds, the famous painter, said: "The more extensive your acquaintance is with the work of those who have excelled, the more extensive will be your own powers of invention; and what may appear still more like a paradox, the more original will be your conceptions."

The Trimmer's Trade for Ambitious Young Men

For the development of a successful automobile trimmer, the most essential requisite is that of neatness. Any one learning the art of trimming must develop first of all an attitude of neatness at all times, both personally and in his work. Cleanliness is a "side partner" of neatness where trimming is concerned.

The surest sign of a capable mechanic is his personal appearance, and the condition of his tools, bench and the work around him. This is particularly true of a trimmer. The cost of materials used and the character of the work demand that these essentials must be a characteristic of the apprentice trimmer.

In connection with this subject we might call the attention of master mechanics and supervisors to the effect that environment has upon an apprentice. If master mechanics would just consider for a moment what lasting impressions had been made upon themselves by certain happenings during their own apprenticeships, influencing them for better or for worse, how much more careful they would be, when apprentices are around, both as to what they say and do.

The condition of the shop, its appearance, system for filing and tabulating patterns, care of materials, personal appearance, condition of tools and benches, topics of conversations, etc.—all affect the present and future progress of the new recruit. The impressions gained by an apprentice are either good or bad, and are lasting. Let us make them for the best.

Looking Into the Future

In considering the advisability of adopting vehicle trimming for a trade, the boy of today should look into the future. The general utility of an automobile, its value for the increase of efficiency, has been proven. As a means of pleasure, nothing has ever equaled it, the industry will go forward by leaps and bounds.

The prospects for the future are most encouraging. The demand for capable trimmers will be greater than ever and the remuneration will be such as to place the vast army of trimmers on the highest plane of successful mechanics, enjoying most of the good things of life. There is every indication that this will prove true and there is every reason why the lad about to enter upon an apprenticeship should carefully consider the art of vehicle trimming before deciding upon a trade or profession.

MURPHY / Duesenberg / CWM

Light, Pleasant, Constructive Work

Vehicle trimming is light, pleasant and constructive work. By this we mean that regardless of the type of car being trimmed, there is nothing laborious about the work, whether it be the finest limousine or a cab for the heaviest truck. It is pleasant because of the variety in types, styles and materials used; constructive because you witness such a vast change in the body as it comes to the trimming department, compared with what it is when completed.

It is always a source of great satisfaction to a trimmer to watch the development of the trimming of a job. It is a real pleasure to see it develop into a work of art, over which the intending purchaser is going to be elated. He is proud that he owns the beautiful work. You are proud because you created it.

The vehicle trimming trade at one time was a seasonal proposition, but it has come about so that it now has no dull seasons. It affords continuous, all-year employment, and it is all indoor work, so that weather conditions do not affect it.

The trimmer's trade gives assurance of a steady weekly return and should not be classed with some of the trades which pay big while you work, but owing to their dependence on weather conditions, etc., do not permit steady, all-year employment. The steady job is far better in the long run.

Another great advantage of this trade is that after having completed an apprenticeship, the field is opened wider to study. There is a never-ending possibility for development of individuality which makes one's services the more desirable and commands greater remuneration the longer one works at the business. Familiarity with colors, their combinations, etc., is a part of this study. Knowledge of kinds of materials, their wearing qualities, etc., is another line of study not learned in a day.

Advantage of a Good Education

We are living in a period of better education and increased efficiency. The education of our youths is much better than in years gone by, and the younger men require different handling. The reasons, why and wherefore of doing certain things must be shown, and in order to be convincing the reasons must be in such shape that they are not only understandable, but also reasonable. By this is meant a "reason for doing it that way" must be shown, and the matter not explained as "it is done that way because it is the way to do it."

Then again, the youth with a good education has a wonderful advantage over those lacking such a foundation. He is able to grasp explanations quickly because his mind has been trained, and his progress will be much greater and faster than those not so fortunate. The value of an education for one seeking to learn automobile upholstery cannot be overestimated.

The Book Teaches the Correct Principles

In this book it will be our aim to cover the field with tolerable thoroughness, explaining the various methods in detail. But the student must bear in mind that the **system** is what he is studying, and that he must not attempt to copy exactly the models as illustrated, because in all likelihood they will not be adaptable in details to the job on which he is working.

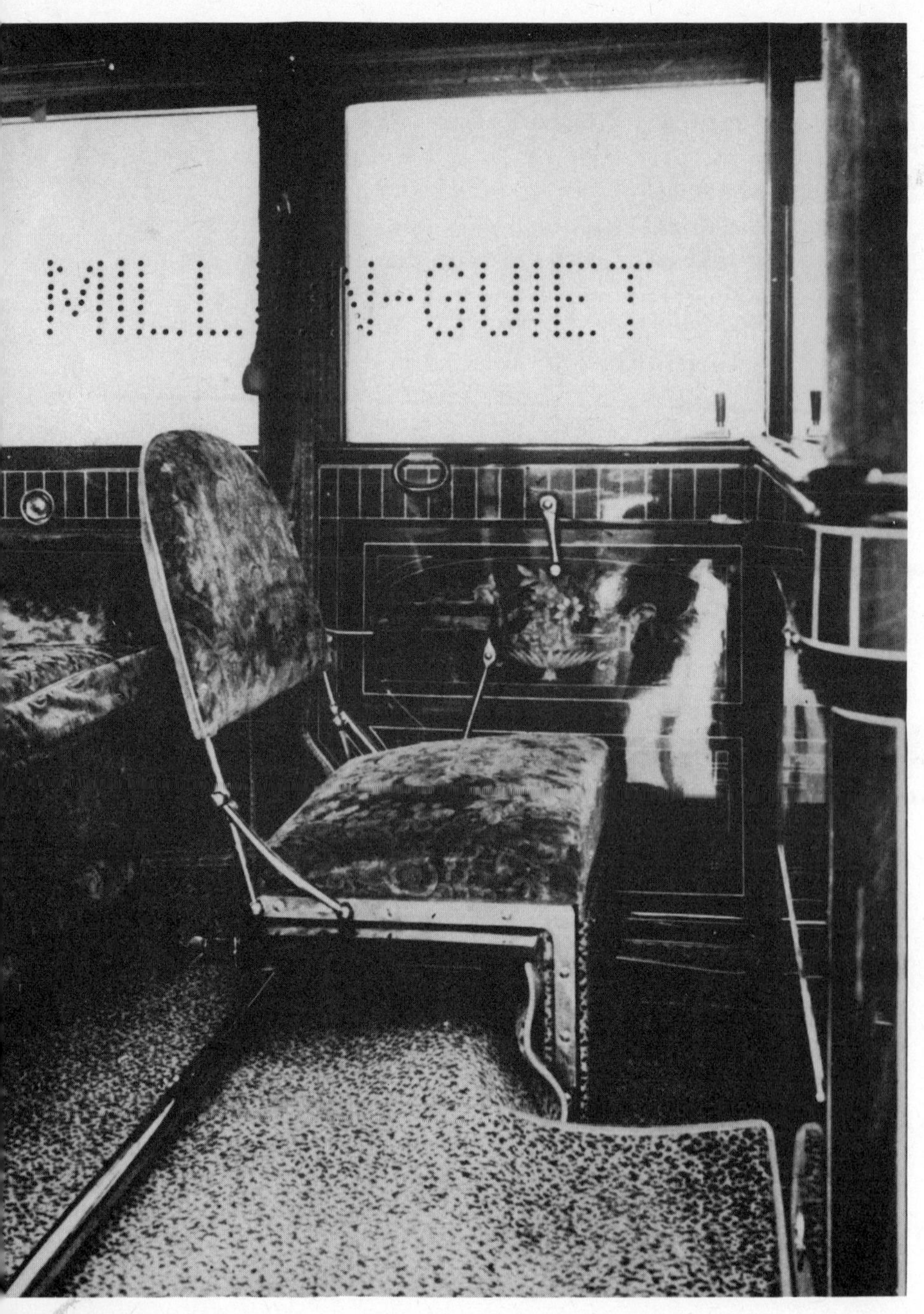

MIL LION-GUIET / Hispano-Suiza /SMacM

CHAPTER II

Getting Acquainted with the Shop

In covering the art of vehicle trimming in this series of articles, it is the purpose of the author to do so in the same manner in which he would handle a young man who came under his charge and who was willing and anxious to learn the art of trimming in its entirety. For that reason we shall at this time enumerate and explain some of the duties of an apprentice when he first enters the business.

Typical Roadster or Runabout

The first duty of the new apprentice will be to become familiar with the shop, the layout of all its departments and to become acquainted with the men in charge. In other words, he must be acclimated.

The new apprentice will be sent on numerous errands around the plant and to the various departments. He will be required to go to the stock or tool room for tools and materials. He will be expected to lend a hand here and there wherever required, doing so with his eyes and ears wide open, to see and observe the various operations in the trimming of the bodies.

Typical Touring Car.

He will be called upon to get a certain tool or piece of material. He must be familiar with their names and know them at a glance. He will be told to get certain patterns

Typical Town Car.

from the files. He must learn the names of these patterns and the part of the body to which they refer. He must learn the names of the various types of bodies and immediately be able to recognize them. He must learn the names of the various parts of the trimming, as used in a body and also the numerous appurtenances used to complete them.

He must learn the names and uses of the various machines and gradually learn to operate them. He must learn to check time against the different jobs and keep records of materials used thereon.

Typical Sedan or Enclosed Drive Car.

All the above an apprentice will be required to master before being permitted to do even some of the least important parts of the work. A bright chap, alert and willing to learn, spends but little time in this preliminary training, and within a few days feels very much at home in the trim shop.

How Patterns are Stored and Filed

One of the important things in trim shop management is to have a convenient method for storing the drawings and patterns, of which there is generally a large accumulation. As any one of these drawings or patterns may be wanted quickly, there must be some system whereby the desired sheets may be found without waste of time.

A very simple, yet easily accessible device for filing drawings and patterns is made in the following manner: Two racks of light lumber, say one-half inch by one-inch strips, are built, forming squares as in Fig. 1.

JUDKINS / Duesenberg / CWM

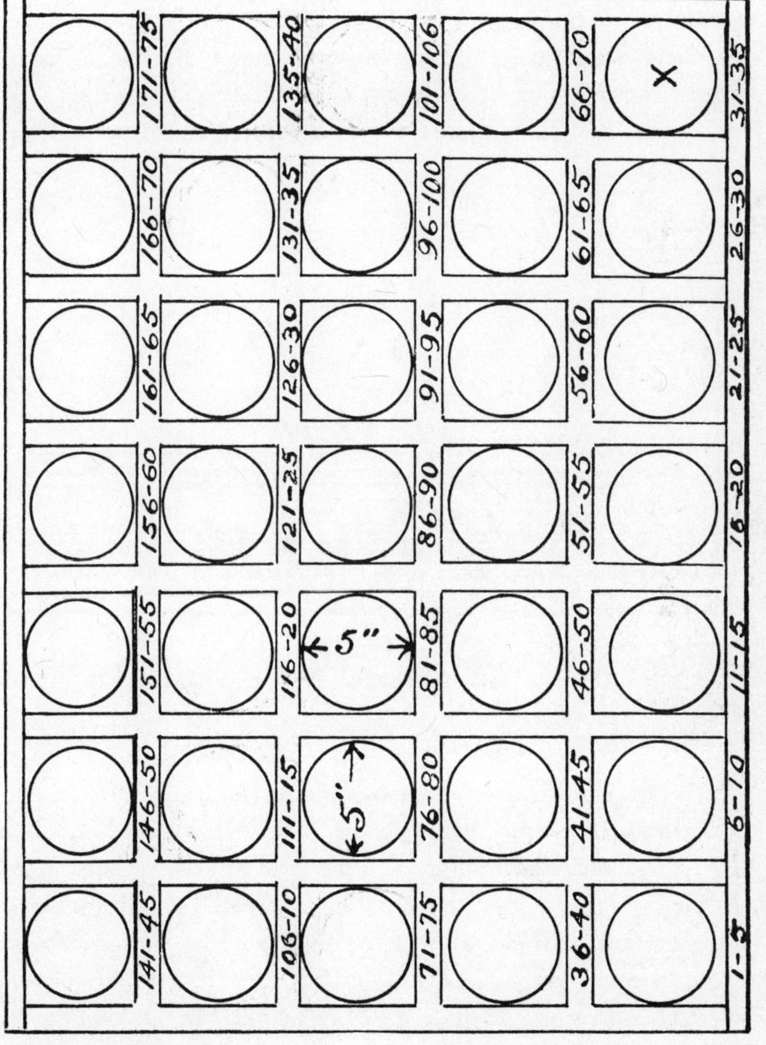

Fig. 1. **Front View of Rack for Filing Drawings, Patterns and Blue Prints.**
(See also Fig. 1a. Side View, on next page.)

These two are then set up with a space between them of thirty inches and securely fastened in this position. Card-board tubes, similar to large mailing tubes, are then placed in each division and numbered, each tube carrying five numbers. Thus a rack of thirty tubes carries one hundred and fifty numerals. A card index is then used for indicating where the pattern or drawing is to be found. The card is made out carrying all the needed information, as in Fig. 2

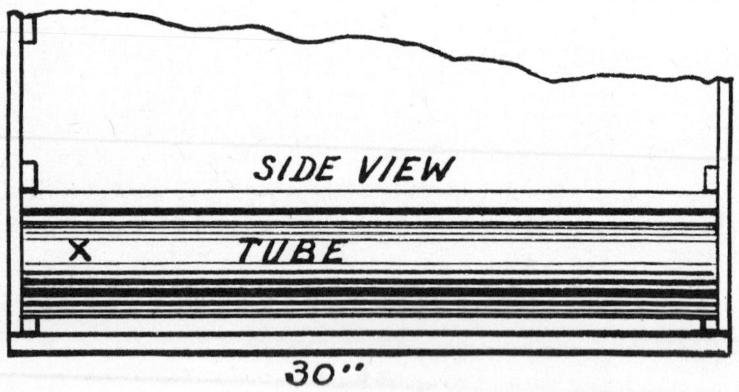

Fig. 1a. Side View of Rack Shown on page 18.

A card would also be made out in the name of Mr. Doe, containing the same information (Fig. 3.) These cards are then filed alphabetically. Then, should it be necessary to duplicate such a job, the card is referred to. It shows the patterns and drawings are filed in tube 33. It requires but a minute to put your fingers on the exact information wanted, and you can find it either under Mr. Doe's name or under the style of body that the trimming was applied to.

Different shops, of course, use different filing systems, but the one described, or something very similar, will be found in most shops where system is a feature.

Packard Limousine 3-35

Built for Mr. John Doe
Trimmed 10/26/18.
Cloth Laidlaw 836
Leather Front—L. G. Bright Black Leather
Style of Trimming, French Plait.

File #33.
Details on Spec. card in file
Job 4627

[Fig]. 2. Index Card for Locating Blue Prints and Patterns as Applied to a Particular Kind of Body. In this case, a Packard Limousine.

Doe, John

Limousine mounted on Packard 3.35
Trimmed 10/26/18
Cloth Laidlaw 836
Leather, Front L. G. Bright Black
Style of trimming—French plait

File 33
Details on Spec. card in file
Job 4627.

Fig. 3. Index Card for Locating a Job Done for a Certain Customer. In this case the customer is John Doe.

Requisition Blanks and Time Cards

All materials and tools, of course, are taken from stock on requisition. Numerous types of requisition blanks are used in various factories, but they must all contain the same information. They must bear the date of requisitioning, the order number of the job or jobs on which the material is to be used, the amount of material, and the signature of the person receiving the material. It has always appealed to the writer to have these requisitions in book form, carrying a carbon copy, permitting of easy reference for the man in charge for checking the materials used.

A Time Card for a Medium-Sized Shop

Where a plant is run on an efficient basis, cost of all work done must be kept. Where the work is not done on piece work or contract basis various methods are in use, some by clock and card system, others by cost clerk in the department and still others by daily work cards, made out by the men themselves, and approved by the foreman in charge. A simple form requiring but little effort and time is shown in Fig. 4

Thus all the workman has to do is to strike a pencil line at the time of starting a job and a line when stopping, marking in between the lines the number of the job on which he worked, as shown in the reproduction. This method is particularly adaptable to the smaller plants and is just as accurate as any other system. The accuracy, of course, is measured by the efficiency of the man in charge. With the above three essentials properly cared for, backed up by the proper supervision, the trim shop is sure to be on the road to efficiency.

The apprentice should get acquainted with all the system cards and blanks used in the shop as early in his career as possible, and adhere to them consistently. System helps to make the shop work move smoothly and also assists you in doing your own particular work.

NAME	John Doe	HOURS WORKED	8
NO. 176	DATE 11/18/18	UNACCOUNTED	✓
ENTERED COST SHEET	✓	TOTAL	8
ENTERED PAY ROLL	✓	LATE OR ABSENT	✓

RATE PER HOUR	.75
RATE PER PIECE	✓
OVERTIME AMOUNT	✓
TOTAL AMOUNT	6.00

TIME	WORK	O. K.
7.00		
6		
12		
18		
24		
30		
36		
42		
48		
54		
8.00		
6		
12		
18		
24		
30		
36		
42		
48		
54		
9.00		
6	4820	3
12		
18		
24		
30		
36		
42		
48		
54		
10.00		
6		
12		
18		
24		
30		
36		
42		
48		
54		
11.00		
6		
12		
18	4815	1
24		
30		
36		
42		
48		
54		
12.00		
6		
12	Lunch	
18		
24		
30		

TIME	WORK	O. K.
36		
42	Lunch	
48		
54		
1.00		
6		
12		
18		
24		
30		
36		
42	4832	
48		
54		2
2.00		
6		
12		
18		
24		
30		
36		
42		
48		
54		
3.00		
6		
12		
18		
24		
30		
36	4817.	
42		
48		2
54		
4.00		
6		
12		
18		
24		
30		
36		
42		
48		
54		
5.00		
6		
12		
18		
24		
30		
36		
42		
48		
54		
6.00		

Fig. 4. Daily Time Card, Filled in by the Workman.

Tools Used in the Trimming Department

Anyone when buying tools should endeavor to buy the best. It always proves to be the cheapest plan in the long run. Tools should always be kept in good working condition. Knives, shears, etc., should be sharp and they should be clean and well adjusted. Each tool should have its place in the kit, and when not in use should be placed there. Then you will know where to find a tool when you need it.

The principal machines used in vehicle trimming are sewing machines of various descriptions, carpet binding machines, tufting machines, button machine, dies for various curtain fasteners, cutting machine, hair picker, eyelet machine, vise and stitching horse. Most of these machines are power-driven. The size and number of these machines vary according to the size of the plant.

Tools Required by the Motor Car Trimmer

In addition to the larger machines mentioned, the trimmer will require a considerable number of special tools as listed:

2-foot Rule
5-foot Rule
5-foot Square (Wood)
6-inch Square (Steel)
24-inch Gauge
24-inch Square (Steel)
Belt Punch
Bevel Square
Brace
Counter Sink
Cutting Pincers
Files
Grommet Punch
Half Moon Needles
Hammers
Hand Drill
Knife
Magnet (for lifting tacks)
Mallet
Monkey Wrench
Oil Can
Patented Tufting Needles
Pliers
Plumb
Reamers up to ¼-inch
Regulators
Sandstone
Sewing Needles
Shears
Small Drills
Spirit Level
Straight Edge (Steel)
Stretchers
Stuffing Rods, various sizes

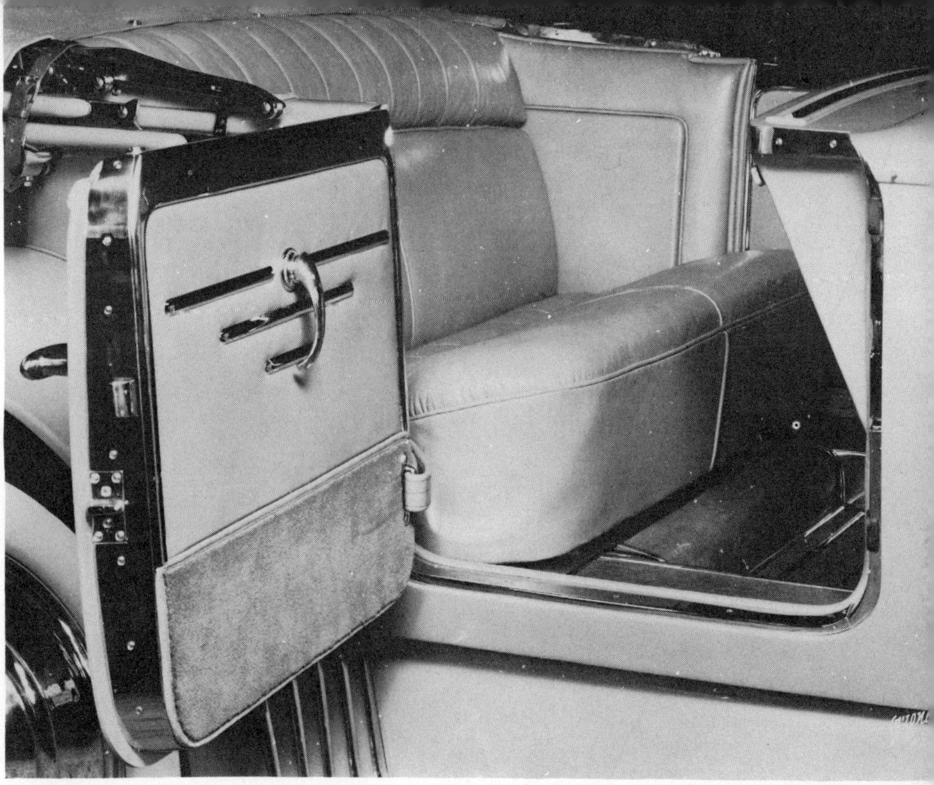

DERHAM / Duesenberg "Tourster" / CWM
WALKER-LE GRANDE / Duesenberg "Torpedo" phaeton / CWM

Telescope Rule
Thimble
Tickler
Tufting Needles
Washer Cutter
Whetstone
Yankee Screw Driver
Yard Stick

Other tools, for which there is not so much use, are:

Awls
Channeling Tools
Creasers
Edge Tools
Gauge Knife
Leather Creasing Machine
Loop Irons, etc.
Pouncing or Stamping Tools
Pricking Wheels
Punches 0 to 1½ in.
Round Knife
Setting-Up Wheels
Slicker
Splitting Knife

The Different Types of Bodies

The young trimmer must make himself acquainted with the different styles of automobile bodies. The list is not a long one, and a short experience in the average shop will soon teach him to identify the leading body types without hesitation.

The various types of bodies are the open touring body, the roadster, the enclosed coupelet, sedan, limousine, landaulet, berlin limousine, collapsible town cars, broughams, and many others. It may take some time to be able to identify all of these styles at sight, but when in doubt ask questions, and you will find your fellow workmen will be glad to give you information. Some manufacturers have invented fancy names for their bodies, but the above list contains the standard names as used by most builders.

The Principal Elements of the Trimming

The names of the principal parts of the trimming and the part of the body to which they are applied are:

Head lining, the inner lining of the roof or top.

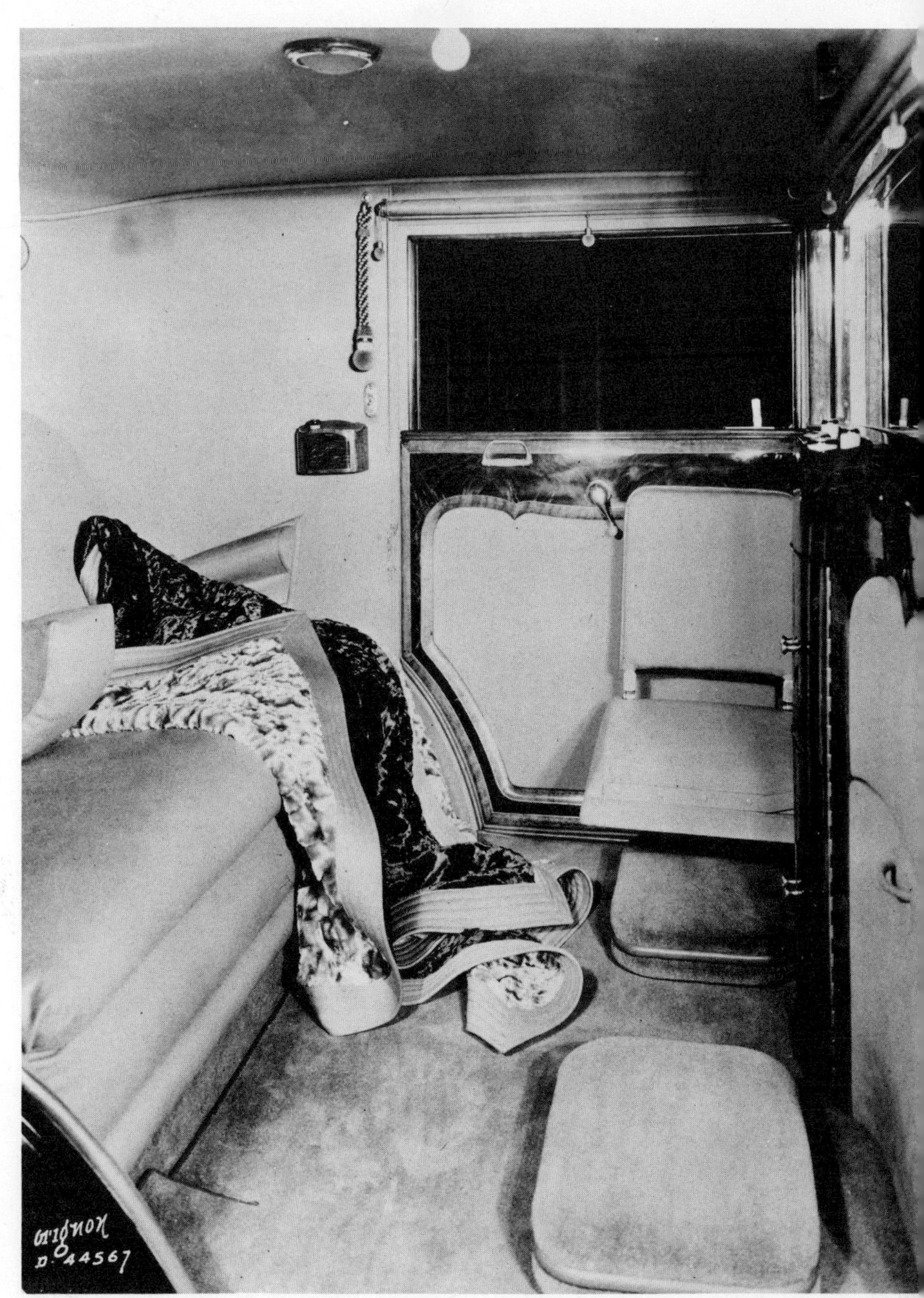

ROLLSTON / Duesenberg / CWM

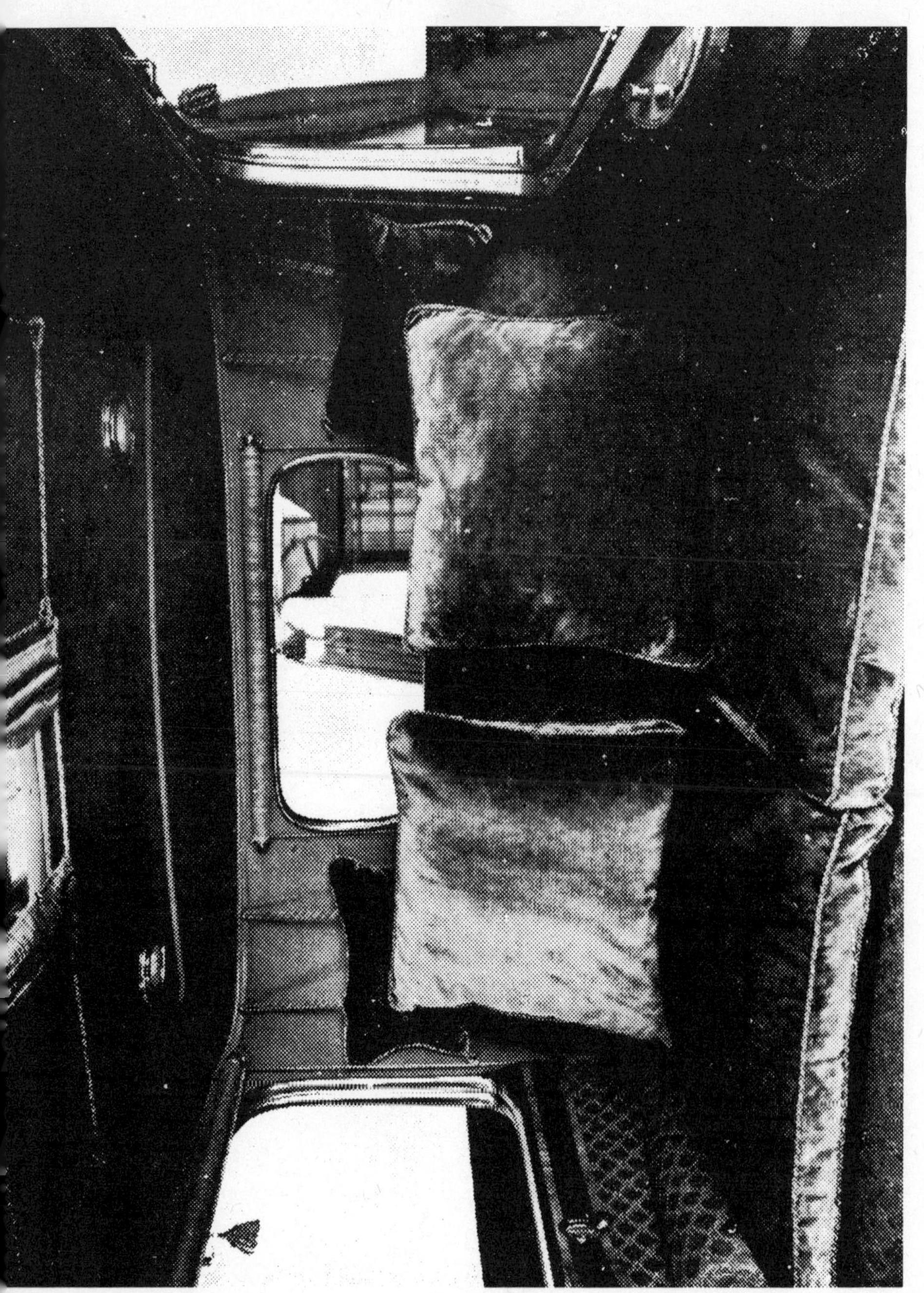

MULLINER / Rolls-Royce / SMacM

Side quarters, being that part of the trimming covering from the rear doors to the back.

Rear back, that part covering the back proper, usually built up over springs.

Rear cushion or seat covering.

The parts of the trimming for a Limousine are:

Anti-Rattlers
Arm Rests
Auxiliary Seats
Bind Nail Combination
Broad Lace
Child Seats
Coupé Pillar
Cowl
Cushion Keeper
Door Checks
Door Pockets
Door Trimming
Draperies
Festoons
Floor Carpet
Foot Rests
Front Back
Front Cushion
Front Door
Front Partition
Front Quarter
Glass Channels
Hassocks
Heel Carpet or Fall
Lazy Back
Molding
Pasting Lace
Robe Rail
Rocker Covers
Roller Curtains
Sash Lifts
Slip Covers
Seaming Cord
Toe Carpet
Welts

The parts of the trimming for a Touring Car are:

Back Curtain
Back Stay
Binding
Bows
Canopy
Cape Top
Cods
Curtain Lights
Deck
Front Valance
Head Lining
Hand Grabs
Imitation Stitch Molding
Joints
Metal Molding
Pads
Quarters
Quarter Pad

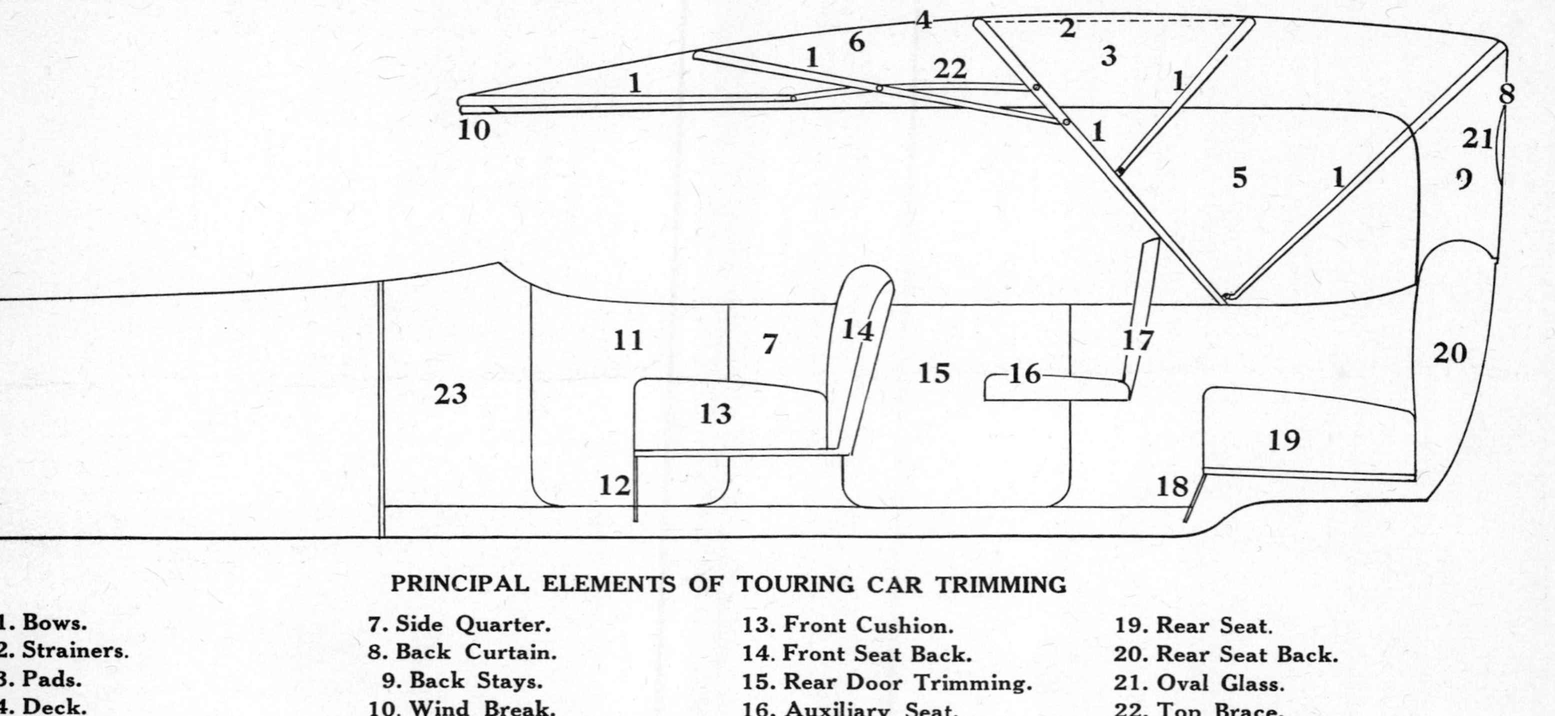

PRINCIPAL ELEMENTS OF TOURING CAR TRIMMING

1. Bows.
2. Strainers.
3. Pads.
4. Deck.
5. Side Curtain.
6. Headlining.
7. Side Quarter.
8. Back Curtain.
9. Back Stays.
10. Wind Break.
11. Front Door Trimming.
12. Front Seat Fall.
13. Front Cushion.
14. Front Seat Back.
15. Rear Door Trimming.
16. Auxiliary Seat.
17. Auxiliary Seat Back.
18. Rear Seat Fall.
19. Rear Seat.
20. Rear Seat Back.
21. Oval Glass.
22. Top Brace.
23. Cowl.

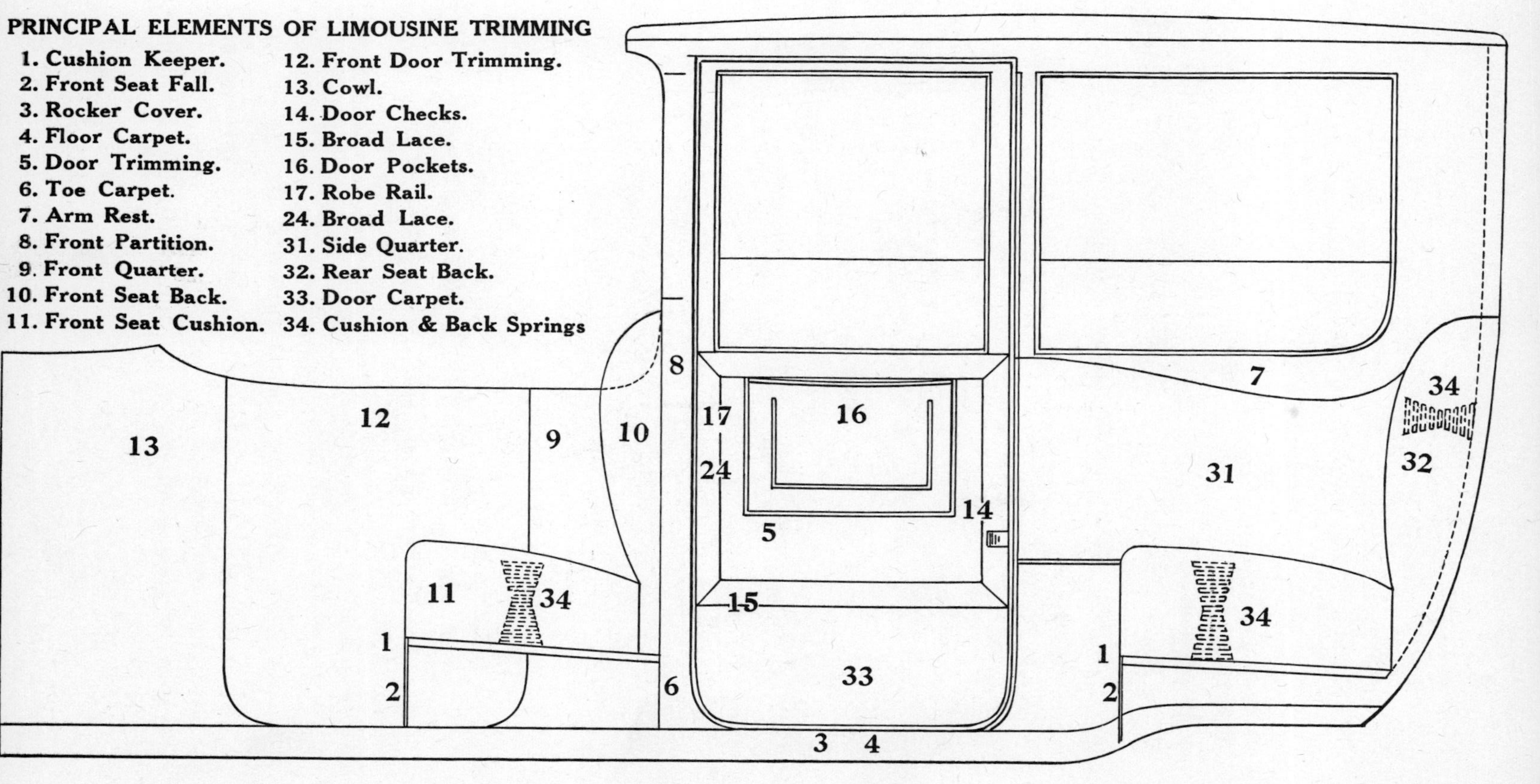
PRINCIPAL ELEMENTS OF LIMOUSINE TRIMMING
1. Cushion Keeper.
2. Front Seat Fall.
3. Rocker Cover.
4. Floor Carpet.
5. Door Trimming.
6. Toe Carpet.
7. Arm Rest.
8. Front Partition.
9. Front Quarter.
10. Front Seat Back.
11. Front Seat Cushion.
12. Front Door Trimming.
13. Cowl.
14. Door Checks.
15. Broad Lace.
16. Door Pockets.
17. Robe Rail.
24. Broad Lace.
31. Side Quarter.
32. Rear Seat Back.
33. Door Carpet.
34. Cushion & Back Springs

Rear Quarters
Rear Valance
Saddle
Side Quarters
Strainers
Victoria Top
Wind Brake
Prop Blocks
Prop Nuts
Shifting Rails
Side Curtains
Sockets
Top Holders
Washers

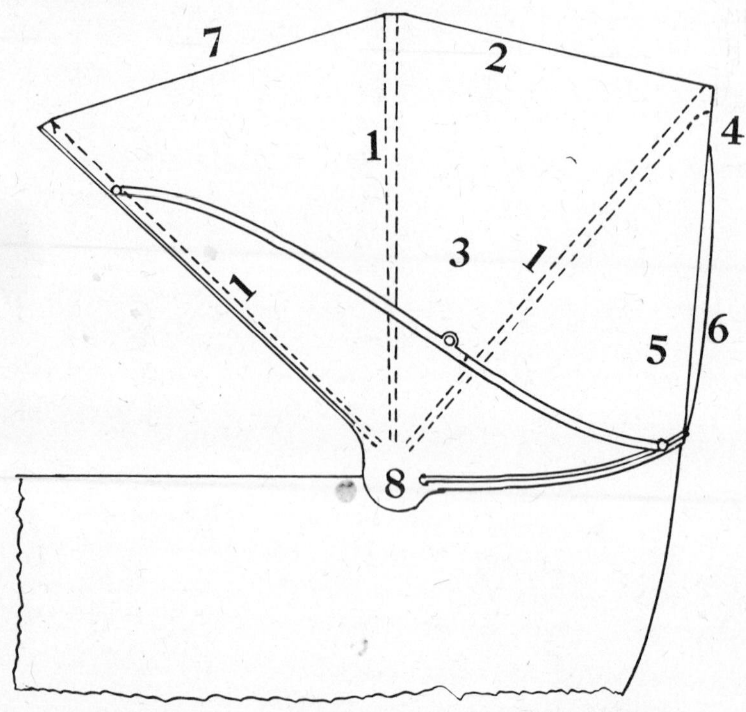

PRINCIPAL ELEMENTS OF A VICTORIA TOP

1. Bows (front, middle and rear).
2. Headlining.
3. Quarter.
4. Back Curtain.
5. Rear Quarter.
6. Back Stay.
7. Deck.

Mountings and Accessories

Then there is a rather lengthy list of parts classified as "Mountings and Accessories," which have a great deal to do with the elegant appearance of modern motor cars. In the selection and application of these parts the trimmer has a fine opportunity to display his good taste or the lack of it.

Acorns
Annunciators
Bouquet Holders
Cigar Lighters
Coat Hooks
Cord Runners
Corner Lights
Curtain Cord
Curtain Rollers
Curtain Screw Eyes
Curtain Sticks
Curtain Wires
Dome Light
Finishing Screws
Finishing Nails
Finishing Washers
Footman Loops
Frogs
Glass Frame Plates
Lace Nails
Landau Curtain
Lever Lock Handles
Luggage Carrier
Megaphone Holders
Pull-to Handles
Roller Supports
Sash Plates
Sash Regulators
Screw Hooks
Screw Knobs
Slide Plates
Smoking Case
Speaking Tubes
Switches
Tabs
Tassels
Telephones
Umbrella Drainers
Umbrella Holders
Vanity Case
Ventilating Knobs
Window Anti-Rattlers
Window Slides

WILLOUGHBY / Lincoln / WEM

CHAPTER III

Motor Car Upholstery Materials

Among the more important materials employed in automobile upholstery are springs, hair and its substitutes, leather and its substitutes, cloth, duck, sheeting, cambric, muslin, buckram, webbing, bow coverings, various sizes and kinds of tacks, nails and brads, escutcheon pins, cotton wadding and batting, down, feathers, top materials, slip cover materials, carpets, velvets, plush, tapestries, silk, linoleum, rubber, celluloid, curtain fasteners, cardboard, silk and linen thread, paste, cement, enameled and coated ducks, moldings, laces, cords and bindings, felt, tufting buttons, and other materials.

The uses to which the various materials are put demands a very close study, as they are the things that in the hands of the trimmer go to make up the complete trimming of the modern motor car.

Seat and Cushion Springs

Springs are used principally in the cushions and backs, serving as shock absorbers and adding to the comfort of the riders.

There are three things that intervene between the road and the occupants of a car which serve to absorb the shocks due to inequalities in the highway. These are the pneumatic rubber tires, the springs upon which the body is mounted, and the upholstery structure, built up of springs and the hair, cotton or other resilient materials, used by the upholsterer or trimmer.

Tires, springs and upholstery all play their part in the designing of a luxuriously comfortable car. A great deal depends on the seat and back springs as to whether or not a job is comfortable, serviceable and durable.

Various kinds of springs may be used. The ordinary spiral may be used with some degree of satisfaction but the durability of such construction is far from being what is expected. Manufactured woven springs, interlaced and bound with metal, are much more satisfactory. Various types of these kinds of springs are made by numerous manufacturers. Patented features are claimed by some makers, but any standard quality, well constructed lace web spring will be found satisfactory.

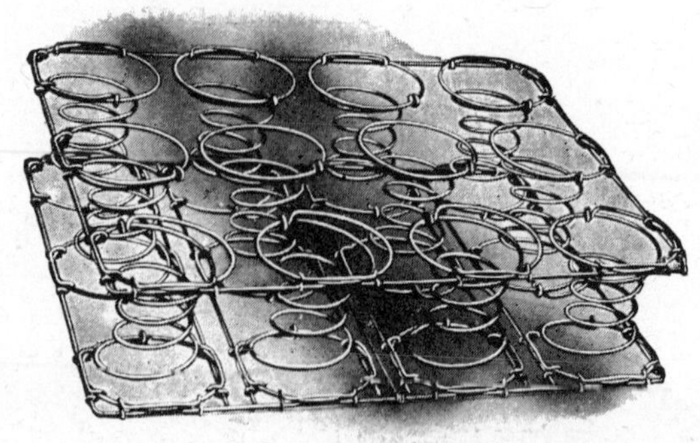

A Typical Spring Seat Construction.

In the making of springs, a great deal of experience is required, for the reason that there are many points to be considered. First the size of the spring for the weight it might be expected to carry, whether one, two or three passengers; second, knowing what the capacity of the springs must be and knowing what height is permitted, experience has taught what gauge wire must be used in the spirals and how many spirals of that particular gauge are necessary to sustain the maximum weight without hitting bottom when "striking bumps" in the road, yet not to be too hard for the minimum weight on smooth roads.

The correct solution of the spring problem is left almost entirely to the spring manufacturer—although certain body builders have a reputation for building hard or soft cushions. Where this is the case the body builder has instructed the spring manufacturer as to the kind of spring he wants. This is often accomplished by having samples made by the spring manufacturer after sufficient information has been given him, and then testing the spring and telling the maker that it is too hard or too soft, leaving the question of gauge of wire and number of spirals entirely to him.

Live, Springy, Genuine Curled Hair.

But, as distinctive characteristics of different body builders are evidenced in the completed job each builder's methods of using a spring foundation must vary. Some firms insist on upholstering with considerable fullness and with heavy toppings on the cushions, while others insist on little fullness and light pads.

These differences of method of course are reflected in the kind of spring used—for instance, on two cushions, each 8 inches high, one with a heavy pad and one with a light pad, the heights of the spring constructions would be different in order to permit the use of the different thicknesses of pads to secure the finished height.

As to the back springs the same principle holds true, but since the purposes of a back spring and a cushion spring are totally different, the springs are also different. We will have something to say about these springs later on in this book.

Cushion Filling Materials

The next important material used in automobile trimming, determining the comfort and durability of a car, is the filling used. Numerous fillings are to be found on the market. Genuine curled hair is generally conceded to be the best. Various grades of hair are to be had, depending generally on the price paid—some hair is hard and stiff; other hair is long and soft, yet has the property of springing back to its original position.

Various interlaced and woven hairs are also used in automobile upholstery. Hair substitutes such as fibre, moss and excelsior, are often used in some grades of work. Recently cotton in its various forms has found many staunch supporters. When using hair the better the hair the surer the satisfaction. But price is not always a criterion for grades of hair. By that it is meant that the more costly hair will often prove the cheaper in the end, due to its greater filling qualities.

Where it is desired to sell the product cheaply, all kinds of substitutes are used for filling, such as fibre, moss, excelsior, etc. This, however, is more particularly true of furniture upholstering. Enameled ducks, drills, etc., are used principally for cushion bottoms and seat board covering, where the boards are not painted. They are also used for linings.

On very special jobs, down and feathers are sometimes used, and then principally for cushions.

Carpets are used principally for floor covering, rocker covering, division covering and heel boards, and the lining of specially arranged compartments, hassocks and foot pads. Linoleum, rubber, etc., are also used for floor covering, heel boards and running boards.

In some styles of trimming both hair and cotton are used for filling. The French plait style is an example of this. Over the spring construction a piece of duck, sheeting, burlap or some similar material is drawn. This being tacked in place, layers of hair are placed, according to the thickness desired.

In some grades of work the interlaced or woven hair is used, being cut exactly to pattern. This of course saves considerable work and assures regularity in cost, because only so many square feet of the product can be used, whereas in laying hair one trimmer will use more or less than another, and his own work will vary. Sheeting, muslin, or some such similar material is then drawn over the hair and tacked or quilted in place. Over this comes the cloth, leather, or leather substitute in which the job is to be upholstered. In the French plait style the plaits or pipes are filled either with hair or cotton, some manufacturers using the double-glazed cotton wadding, some the cotton batts and others hair.

Tacks and Their Uses

Tacks for automobile upholstery are made in great varieties and each style serves its particular purpose best. The styles mostly used in trimming are upholsterers' Swedish iron tacks, lace tacks, gimp tacks, lining nails, saddle nails, and escutcheon pins. The various styles are made in numerous sizes and the big secret in the use of tacks is to use a large enough size to properly hold the work in place, but not to use a ten-ounce tack where a three-ounce tack is sufficient. The Swedish iron tacks are used generally on foundation work where they are not seen in the finished production. The others are used in various finishes and their names are very suggestive of the uses to which they are put in motor car upholstery work.

Buckram

Buckram is an essential material in automobile upholstering, being made in single, double, and three-ply. It is used for reinforcing and backing, for "pasting out," such as doors, flaps, wind-brakes and for a foundation on which springs are sewed for back spring construction, where springs are made up by the trimmer. It is often used for closing in open spaces between strainers or on any part of a job where a more solid backing is required. Owing to its many uses buckram is an indispensable article in the trimming department. It possesses long life and much durability; yet on the cheaper grades of work cardboard is often used for the same purposes.

TOP CONTAINER BUILT INTO THE BODY
This English device preserves the graceful lines of the body when the top is down, the top being entirely concealed from view.

Celluloid or "pyralin," is used mainly for vision lights on touring car tops or for similar use on collapsible cape tops. It also makes an admirable binder and edging for "blind" or concealcd tacking.

Cloths used in upholstering are of many varieties, such as broadcloths, whipcords, diagonals, tapestries, plushes, velvets, linens, Bedford cloths, etc. They are of varied colors, figures, textures and weaves, but the better grades are made exclusively of wool and the softness of the materials adds to the comfort of the job. The colors and designs tend to

SAOUTCHIK / Delage / SMacM

enhance the beauty of the interior. Leather and its substitutes are used for upholstering types of cars more directly subject to hard wear and weather exposure, such as the roadster and touring car.

Real leather, that is, hand-buffed top grain leather, is often used in high-grade bodies. Upholstering and top leathers are usually made from cow hides, but goat skins and pig skins are also used. Price considered, leather substitutes answer the same purposes, especially when price is a consideration. Leather substitutes today are made in a variety of finishes and colors and are found quite durable. They may be cleaned exactly the same as leather, are water proof and are not liable to crack or peel.

Grain leather is used also for top coverings, such as Victoria tops, town cars, landaulets, etc. Leather substitutes made for the purpose are adaptable for the same uses. Leather substitute manufacturers are also making special coverings for touring tops, etc.

Cleaning Upholstery Materials

It is well here to call attention to the fact that dirt is the worst enemy of any kind of upholstering material. Since automobiles are subject to considerable dust and dirt, the proper method of cleaning should be known. Gasoline should never be used on any kind of upholstering, particularly leather and its substitutes, as it tends to harden the surfaces. Before using any cleaning fluid, the upholstering should be well brushed. On leather and its substitutes a wash with castile soap and lukewarm water is the proper cleansing method, drying thoroughly. Treating with neatsfoot oil or sweet oil will preserve and soften the material. For leather substitutes there are numerous dressings on the markets, most of which are very good, but they should not be used until the substitute has been properly cleansed with lukewarm water in which some castile soap has been dissolved.

Other grades of leather besides the trimming and top

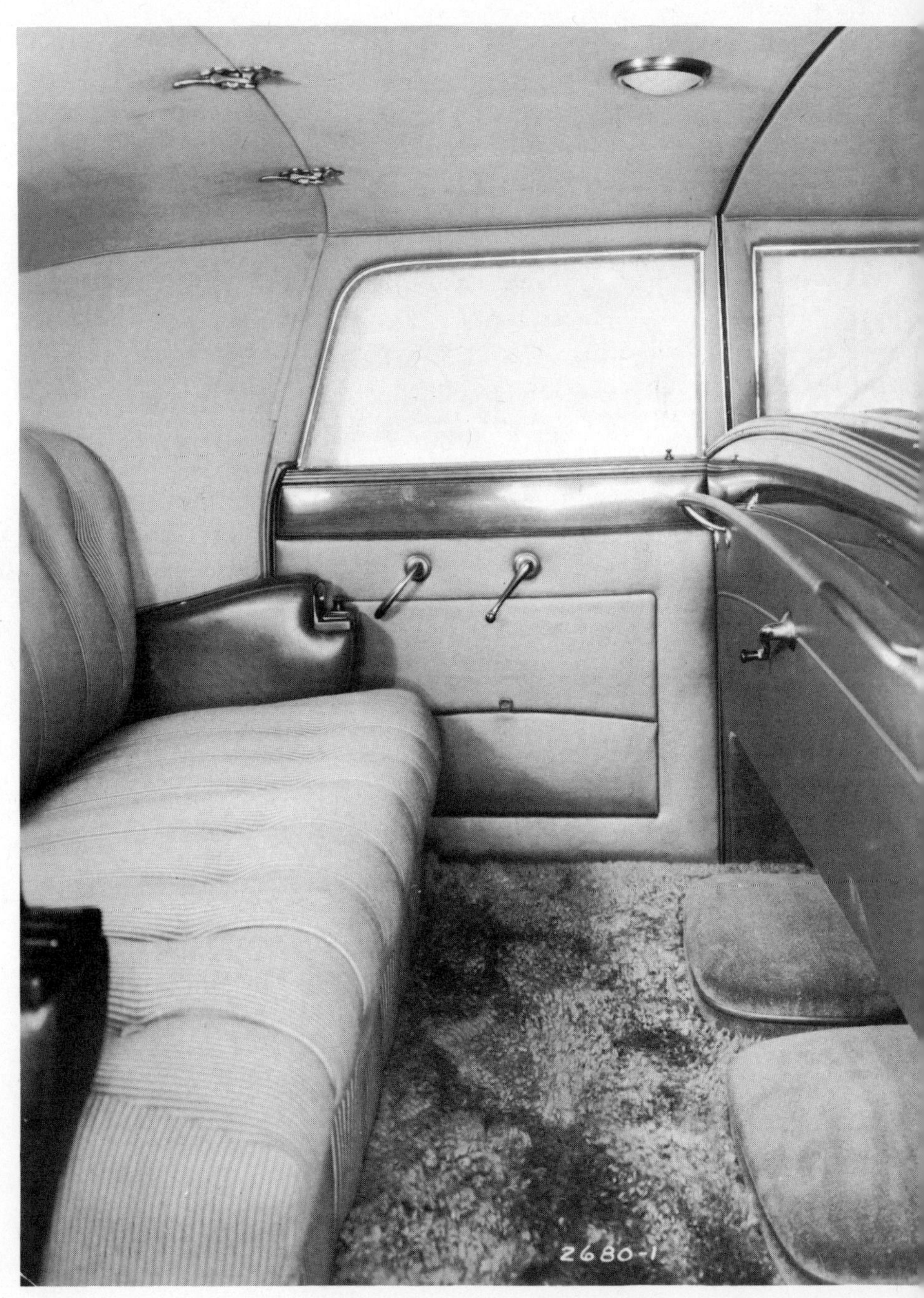

BRUNN / Lincoln / WEM

leathers are used in automobile upholstering. Both harness and dash leathers are used by trimmers. Harness leather is used principally for straps, foundations for robe rails, door checks or other reinforcements, which are subject to excessive strain. Dash leather is used principally for dashes, fenders, valences, etc.

Special worsted and silk laces, cords, bindings and broad laces are also used, which are manufactured for the purpose. They are used principally to "finish off" the job. Laces, cords and bindings are also made extensively of the materials in which the job is upholstered.

Moldings of various kinds, principally lead filled, blind nailed, are sometimes used for finishing on outside surfaces, either covered with the material used in upholstering, plated or painted. Silk for roller curtains, festoon curtains and draperies are made specially for this purpose to match the various cloths sold for upholstering, 27 inches is the most adaptable width for this purpose.

Other appurtenance manufactured specially to match the cloth are, tassels, handgrabs, sash lifts, robe rails, luggage cords, hat racks, curtain cords and acorns. In connection with automobile upholstering many materials are manufactured specially for certain purposes such as coverings, webbings, gimps, curtain fasteners, curtain lights, footman loops, top fasteners and clamps, pull-to handles, lever lock handles, cap screws, vanity and smoking cases, interior lights and fittings, all of which serve their purposes well, adding to the beauty and comfort of the car and to the pleasure and satisfaction of the purchaser.

Automobile Carpets

Rug making in well-regulated shops is not handled in the body trimming shop. Patterns are made, a sample rug is gotten ready and fitted in the job to prove the pattern. Then, if the pattern proves correct, the amount of carpet is cut to fill the order and the binding and operating is done in the operating room.

Making carpet for custom work should be done in this manner: The pattern is fitted to the job, carpet cut according to pattern and fitted in the job to prove its fit.

For limousine work the carpet should always be lined. The reasons for lining are, first to stiffen the carpet, secondly to keep road dirt from penetrating the back of the carpet.

Very often the lining is pasted solidly; sometimes the carpet is laid on the lining and sewed around before binding; sometimes there is a piece of cotton used as a padding.

The carpet is bound with the well-known round binding, but frequently in high-class work we create a French binding, which is done by sewing a line on top of the binding at either edge, thus making a flat binding and adding strength to the work. Where the French binding is used it is necessary to cut the pile of the carpet where the binding is done, thus allowing a flat finish.

On the cheaper grades of work in factory outputs a binding machine is used. On custom work the binding is of the same material as the trimming used. There is also a regular manufactured binding of worsted goods the same color as that of the goods in which the job is trimmed. Also where worsted lace is used the carpet may be bound, turning the face over by hand. Often, the pile of the carpet where the binding takes place must be cut down.

Binding with flat lace is done in this manner: Sew the bottom of the flange to the carpet first, all around where it is to be bound, turning the lace over by hand or basting, and sew close to the edge by machine. This also creates a flat binding and is extremely neat.

The same system is followed in the making of carpet rocker covers. They may be cut in numbers and be ready to be placed in the job while at the trimmer's bench. In placing the rocker covers in the job, where radius or shape varies, wetting the carpet on the back and using paste in assembly is necessary.

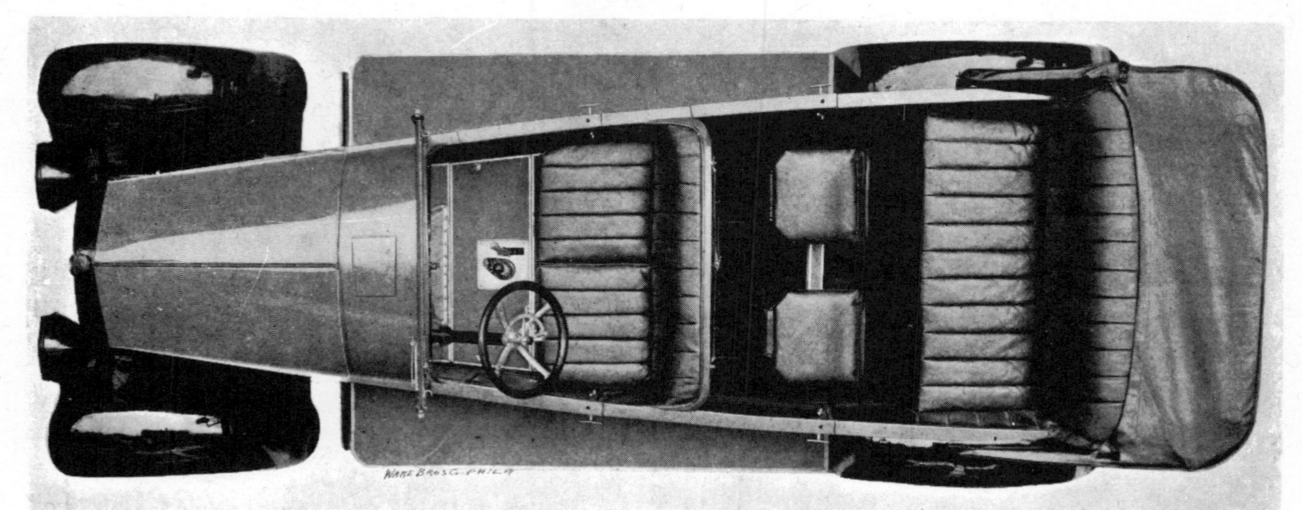

TOP VIEW OF A TOURING CAR, SHOWING FRONT SEATS, REAR CUSHION AND TWO AUXILIARY OR FOLDING SEATS.

In the French plait style of motor car upholstering the plaits of the cushion must line up exactly with the plaits of the back, making a continuous line. In the example shown above the lining up is faulty, giving a poor appearance.

CHAPTER IV

Laying Out the Work

In the laying out of all work harmony must exist. Symmetry of lines must be characteristic of the work. For example, in the French plait style, the plaits of the cushion must line up with those of the back, making a continuous line, as if they were one and the same line drawn to a continuation. Method in doing the work is absolutely essential, and a simple process is that of working from the center at all times and strictly adhering to the measurements on the patterns and drafts.

The Different Styles of Trimming

The making of patterns is the foundation for the construction of the completed job, and in the making of patterns and drafts the greatest care should be taken. They should be correct in the first place and then strictly followed.

In the laying out and making of patterns we shall treat the following styles: French plait, diamond tufting in connection with piping, biscuit or block tufting, negligee and absolutely plain work. These constitute the styles of the past, the present and the future, used in all styles of work and in all kinds of upholstery, and will be so used for years.

These are the general styles used and are practically the only styles adaptable to automobile upholstery, so consequently we are using these styles as adaptable to the future as well as to the past and present. Many variations of the above-mentioned styles are used, but fundamentally they are the foundation of all automobile upholstery.

Difference in methods and in their application varies with the individual production. As systems are generally individual, the methods and systems used by the writer are also to a certain extent individual. While they may not be received as authoritative, they will be used as demonstrative of up-to-date methods and instructive to the apprentice as well as to the workman at the bench.

The methods used in demonstrations, as well as the drawings shown, will be made as plain as possible, as well as the ways of doing the work and the making of patterns, taking always into consideration simplicity and cost of production. Further individuality must be left to the imagination and the practical skill of the reader.

Let us take up some of the details of laying out the work, the making of patterns and doing the work in detail, taking up each individual part separately and completing each portion of the job. We will first take up the laying out of patterns and the making of drafts for each section of trimming where required.

Whereas, in custom shops only the principal patterns are made, such as cushion, back and doors, in shops where large output is required patterns are made for every part requiring the cutting of fabrics, for the reason that it is productive of the saving of much valuable material.

As we are illustrating the making of patterns, we will begin with the making of patterns for each individual part of the trimming of a Touring Car. First, would be the making of the patterns for the cushions and back springs, since these patterns must be sent to the spring manufacturer and the springs must be on hand when the job is ready to trim.

In connection with the making of patterns and the initial work of trimming a body, it may be mentioned here that apprentices and beginners can be used to good advantage in the cutting of foundation materials, "roughstuff," etc., and the pasting out of various parts, in order that they become thoroughly familiar with the patterns and parts. This applies more particularly to the custom shop, because in large factories the teaching of the trade in its entirety is not usual.

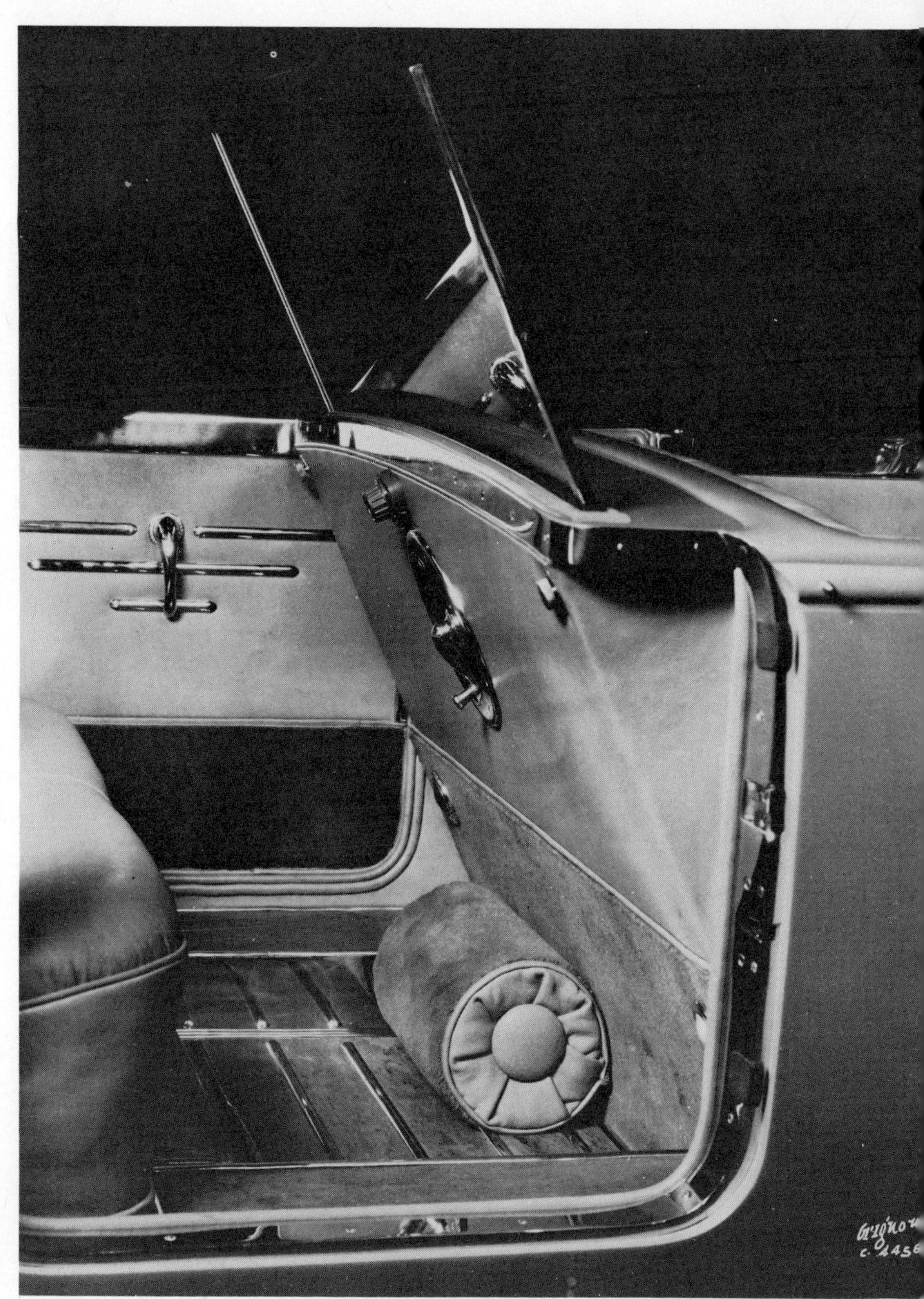

DERHAM / Duesenberg "Tourster" / CWM

More often, in the larger shops, specialists are trained for each particular operation, such as cutting; operating (usually females); pasting out and cementing (usually females); back making; back hanging; cushion making; tacking in head lining and above belt line (enclosed bodies); rug making, which is done from patterns; top making; slip covering, etc.

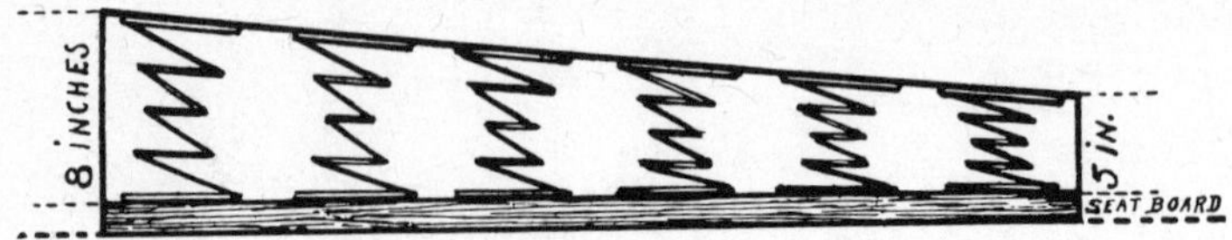

Correct Method, Three-Inch Pitch to the Rear.

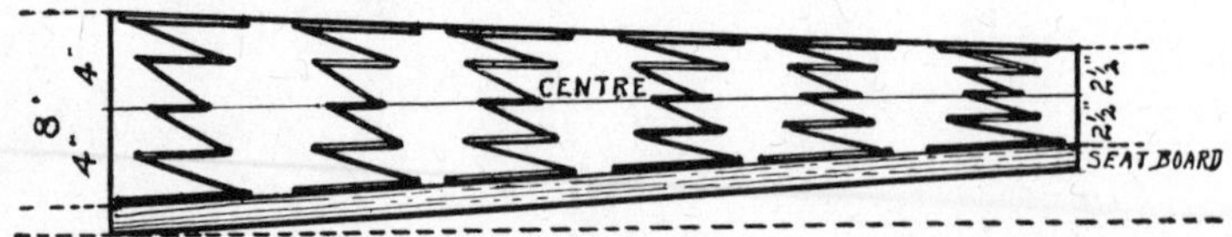

A Spring Made in this Manner has no Top or Bottom, and is Incorrect. When Placed in Position it will Give a Result as in the Next Diagram Below.

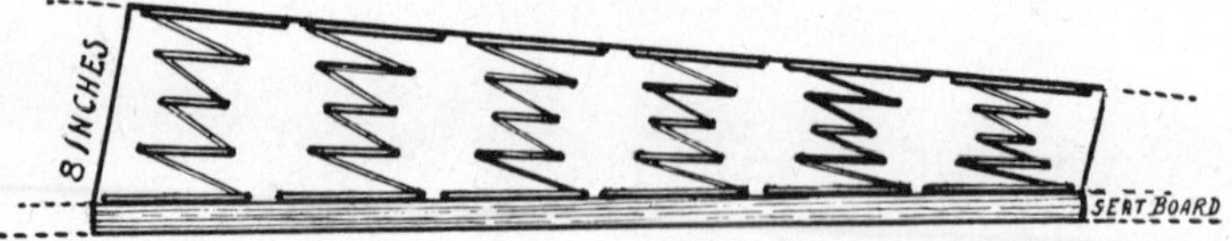

Incorrectly Designed Spring as it Appears When Placed in Position.

Fitting and Making Cushion Spring Pattern

The manner of making and fitting patterns for a touring car cushion spring will be adaptable for any other type of body after allowances are made for thickness of side quarters and back. In fitting the pattern the thickness of quarters and back must be anticipated for the reason that different types of cars require different sizes of backs and cushions. This is mentioned only as a precaution. As a usual thing the method of fitting which we explain will be suitable to follow in almost any type or style of trimming. We are endeavoring to explain the most simple and accurate method possible, bearing in mind the fact that it is but an example.

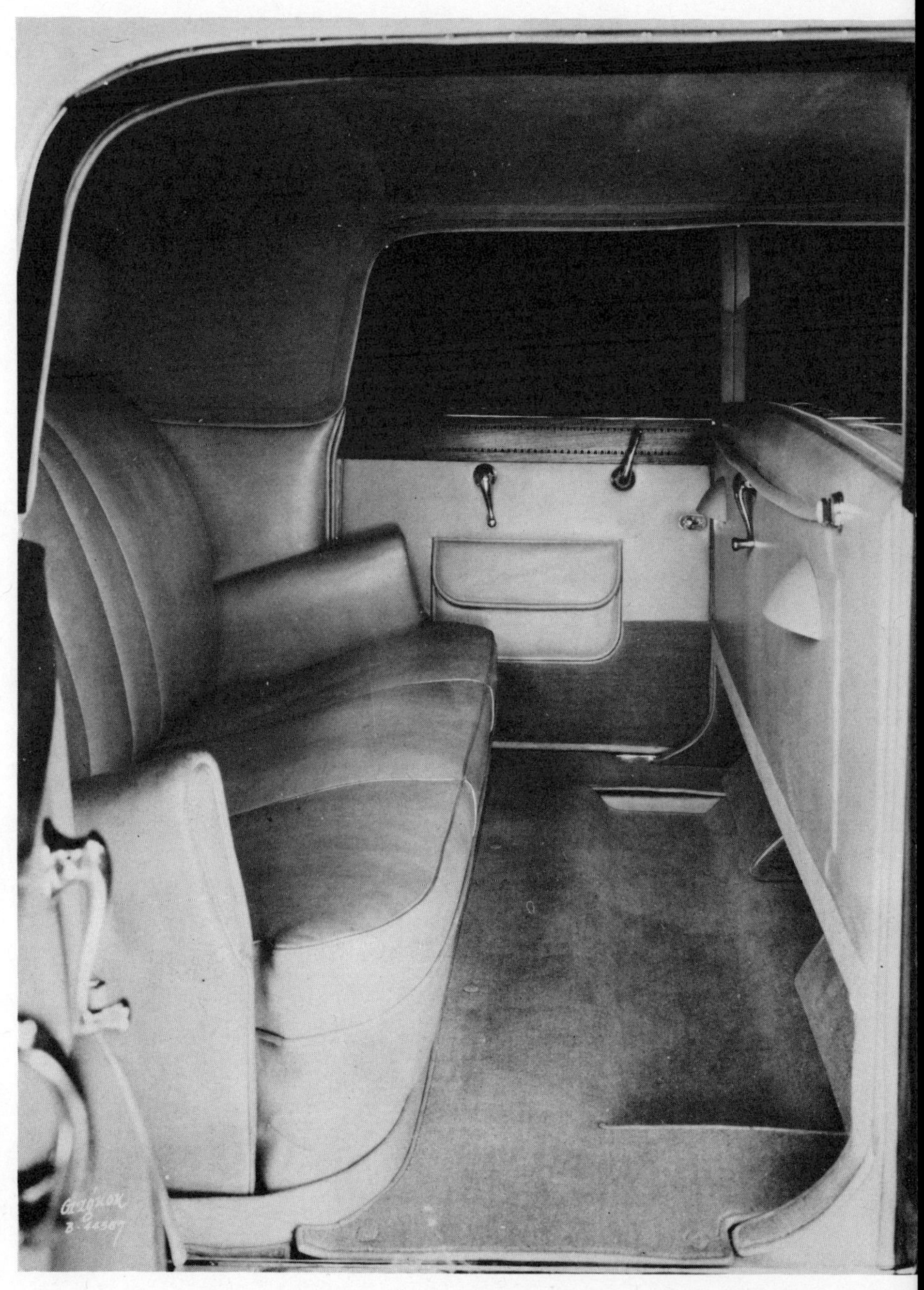

ROLLSTON / Duesenberg / WCK

After being first assured that the blocking out is as intended for the particular style of trimming, we will take a piece of paper, cheap canvas or other suitable material, cut of sufficient size, tack temporarily to keep the material used from slipping, mark at the front edge of the seat board and mark accurately around the blocking at the quarters and at the back.

The back, when built permanently in the job, is going to take up from one inch to one and one-half inches where it comes in contact with the cushion. If we find that the construction of the back will fill out one inch or one and one-half inches when finished we must allow that amount of reduction for the size of the cushion spring pattern at this point. These deductions we find are about the average amount of space taken up by the back.

The same consideration should be taken up at the quarters, but the quarters do not take up as much space as the back, and we find that the average is one-half to five-eighths of an inch.

All allowances are made for all the room taken up by the back and quarters and all allowances for the space taken up by the completed cushion. This gives sufficient amount of room when the cushion is finished so that it will not bind at any point.

We must also take into consideration the rounded corners at the rear and sufficient radius must be given at these rear corners, otherwise the cushion will bind at these points and spoil a well-intended pattern.

In making the pattern the height is of the utmost importance. In arriving at the proper height of the spring we have the thought in mind of the measurement from the floor to the top of the seat. For instance, from the floor boards to the top of the seat boards is four inches. The highest measurement for comfort in a cushion should not exceed fifteen inches; therefore, we find a difference of eleven inches and we find that our pad will finish at three inches, so after the deductions are made we discover that our spring must not exceed eight inches in height at the front.

A pitch or decline is necessary in the shape of springs, and trimmers have found that the average big car is most comfortable with a pitch of three inches. So we arrive at the conclusion that our spring shall be eight inches high in front and five inches high at the rear. Later-day body construction usually permits that the spring be made square up all around. By this is meant square up from the seat board. The illustration shows the correct way for the making of a spring. (See diagrams on page 58.)

At all times the gauge of the wire used is that adaptable to the carrying capacity of one, two or three passengers. This gauge is usually left to the spring maker, after noting on your pattern the uses to which the cushion will be subjected, but at all times the spring should be of sufficient gauge to take the bumps and jars of road driving. Some manufacturers require an unusually soft cushion, while others are not so particular, so consequently this is arrived at by the requirements of the builder. We believe that we have made clear the average method required in the making of a spring and pattern.

Making Patterns for the Back Springs

Back springs have probably a greater variance than the cushion springs and there are many different styles of back spring constructions now in use. There are division backs or divided backs for one, two and three passengers, but at this time we will treat the construction of the single back spring.

When making the pattern for the back spring we must take into consideration the thickness that the finished quarters will take up, the height of the finished cushion and the thickness the back is to be when finished. We are treating of the lace web style of spring construction for the back as well as for the cushion. However, many manufacturers require that the back springs be made up of spiral springs sewed to buckram in the trimming shop, but there are many advantages in using the manufactured springs.

We must allow enough "play" or clearance at the side quarters so that the back spring will not bind, which would cause it to buckle toward the center, thus allowing a sinking in of the back.

The Cushion Spring

The cushion spring that we have just made is to be five inches in height when finished, so we must make that deduction for the back spring at the bottom. Allowing for trimming, the spring should set about seven inches from the floor, one inch from the quarter and be even at the top at the framework on a body. The height of backs vary, but these measurements being followed usually, we have a comfortable, well-working back.

Patterns should be made from the same material as that which is used for making of the cushion pattern. Duplicate patterns should always be kept on file so as to prove the correctness of the manufacturer's delivered spring, and for future reference.

We have used this method of making spring patterns with the thought in mind of demonstrating as an example the French plait style of upholstery, where the work of finishing is done over the springs themselves, yet the springs are adaptable for tufted, negligee or plain work, which styles will be discussed further on.

Methods of Fitting Doors

For custom work, where the size of doors that have not been made to forms will vary, it is necessary to make patterns for each door, especially where anything but plain trimming is used. The patterns should be made from paper, marking accurately around all the outer edges, then laying out for the pockets and flaps, from which the buckram or cardboard foundation is taken. Allowances should be made and deducted from the outer edges for the width of the laces or other finishes that may be used. This explanation will apply to almost any style door trimming.

BRUNN / Lincoln / WEM

Foundation for the Cushion, French Plait Style

The spring pattern having been previously made and having kept a duplicate at hand, we must order made a wood frame on which the spring is to be attached. We are using the wood frame for the reason that it is most adaptable to rapid work, and also for the reason that it always keeps the cushion permanently in position.

AN UNUSUAL DOOR TREATMENT.
Showing rubber-gathered velvet pockets in door and concealed under the flaps. A closed car convenience.

The wood frame should be made about four inches in width, seven-eighths of one inch in thickness, to the exact size of the spring pattern. The spring is attached to the wood frame with three-quarter-inch galvanized iron staples

LOCKE / Duesenberg / CWM

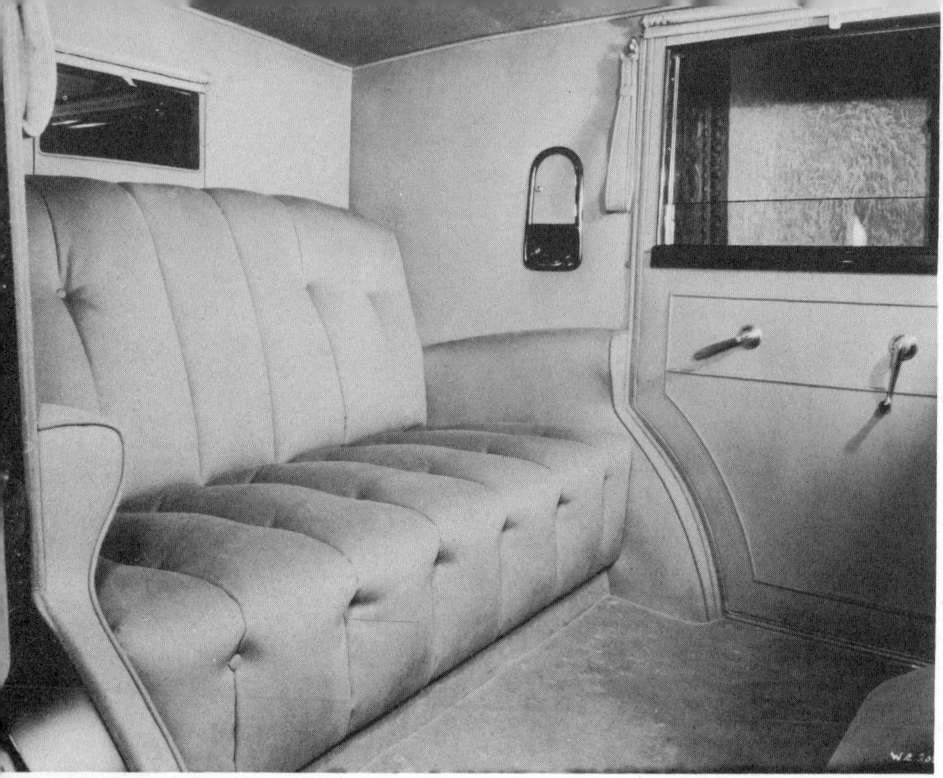

BRUNN / Lincoln / WEM
WILLOUGHBY / Lincoln / WEM

and assures that the spring is firmly attached. The wood frame gives the means of firmly holding the trimming in position.

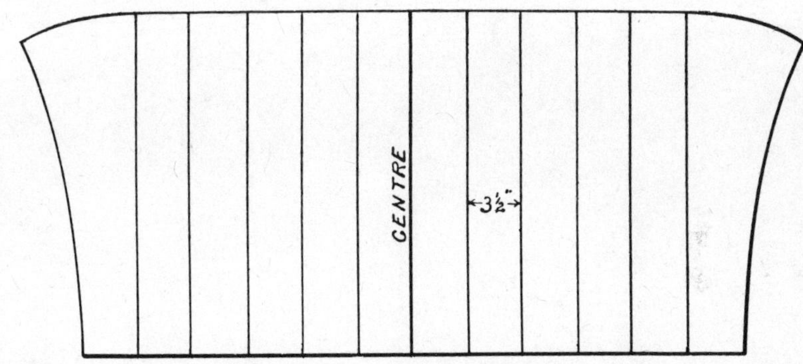

Foundation Pattern for Back—French Plait Style.

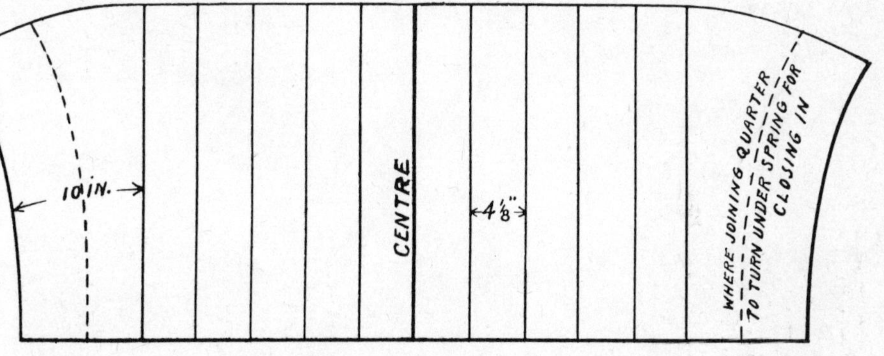

Fullness Pattern, Which is Just an Enlargement Over the Foundation Pattern; the Fullness, When Sewed to the Foundation, Leaves Room for Filling.

The top, or rather the entire spring, is covered with a piece of ten-ounce duck or other suitable material, tacked to the wood frame around the outer edges. A roll is then sewed one and one-half inches from the outer edges of the spring by "shot stitching," or this covering may be fitted and the roll sewed on by machine. That is, the inner part; or a manufactured roll, may be sewed around the sides and front. Stitch strings across, under which the hair is placed, topped off lightly with hair. A covering of five-ounce sheeting is put over the hair, stretched tightly and smoothly.

BRUNN / Lincoln / WEM

Quilting is often necessary. It should be then stitched all around under the spring edge, that is, the top spring edge.

The top part is now ready for the trimming proper, but the strain should be taken from the spring, that is to say, the covering that we have already placed over the entire spring should be left free around the sides; then tacked permanently around the wood frame at the bottom of the spring. The cushion is now ready for the outer covering.

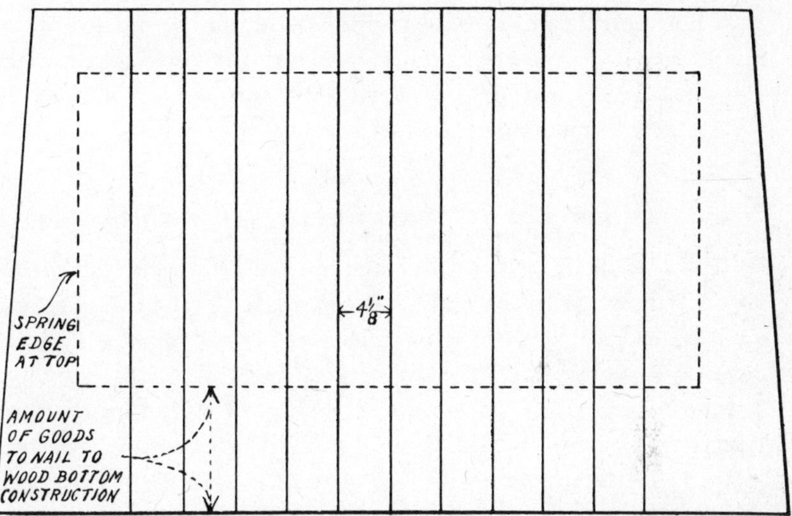

Fullness Pattern for Cushion. The Foundation Pattern Would be the Same as Above, Reduced Five-eighths Inch Between Each Vertical Line.

Foundation for the Backs

In forming the foundation for the back (the making of the spring and patterns having been previously described) the spring is placed in position in the job and is covered with a suitable spring covering of ten-ounce duck or other material and the goods are sewed to the spring after being placed in the proper position. Over this is placed another covering of the same material, and across the bottom, above the cushion line, a line of sewing is made, allowing on the sides a sufficient amount of material to turn in, thus forming a pocket.

The hair is either strung in and topped off, or pushed in by hand until the desired shape is attained. The outer covering is drawn up and the hair is then quilted to keep its shape. The utmost care should be taken that the back is built to the required measurements of the draft.

This is a simplified method of building the foundation for a back of the French plait style of work, and it has proved to be satisfactory and is used by many of the best body manufacturers.

A pad can be made on a frame at the bench, but the first-mentioned method permits a more rapid production and at a less cost, and proves very satisfactory. The back is then ready for its outer covering.

Foundation Patterns for Outer Covering, French Plait Style

The foundations for the back and cushion having been described, we will now take up the making of patterns and the method of handling the outer covering for the French plait style of work.

Making the patterns for the French plait style in a cushion shop, or in a shop where large production is required, is the feature we are attempting to describe. In order to get correct patterns, this method must be used in either case, for we must build our foundation before the correct pattern can be arrived at.

To make the pattern proper for the outer covering, we must take a piece of pliable goods which can be used for the completed section, or, we mean to say, that if we are building a custom job the same goods used in making the pattern will be used for the foundation, hence there is no waste.

Stretch the goods firmly over the part to be fitted—the cushion, the backs or the quarters—and temporarily tack. The cushion, for instance, is covered in its entirety over the foundation which has been mentioned. Mark around the outer edges of the top, and the four corners of the wood frame at the bottom, marking the centers accurately front

BRUNN / Lincoln / WEM

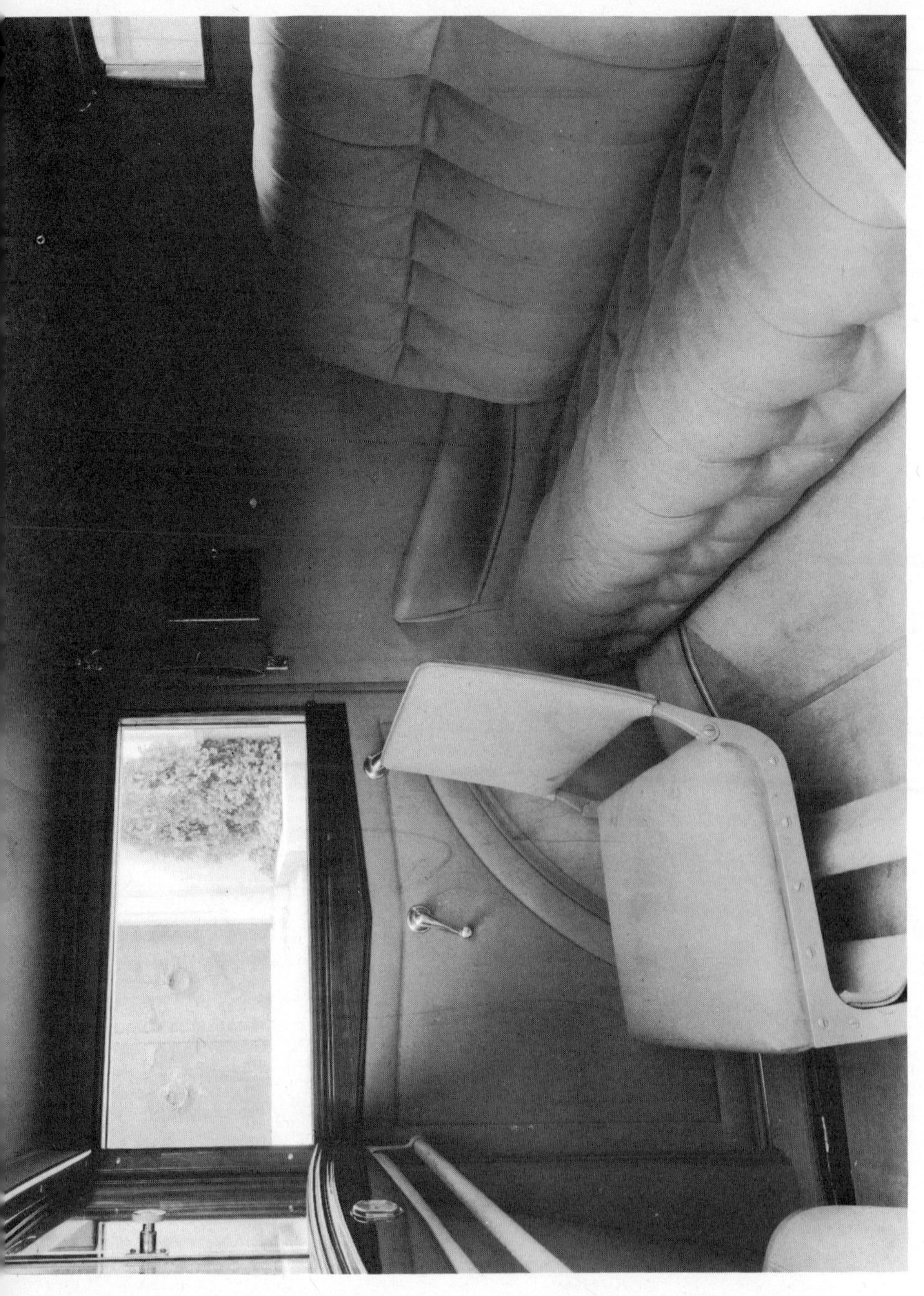

ROLLSON / Packard / WEM

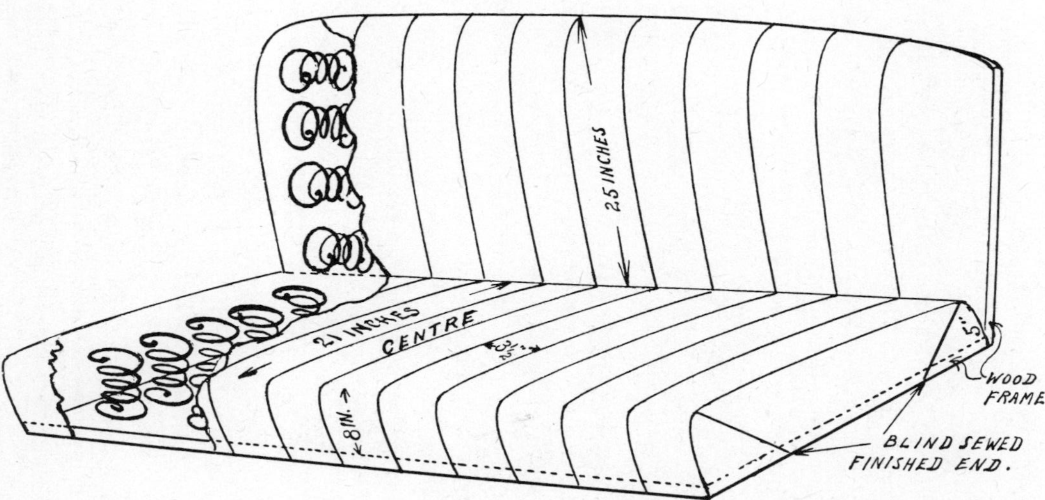

Rear Cushion and Back, Showing How Lines of the Back Cushion are Brought to a Perfect Alignment with Those of the Seat Cushion. Compare This Drawing with the Photograph of a Touring Car Shown on Page 54

and back; take up; lay on the bench; space off in the manner illustrated in the drawing.

We have spoken in the first part of this chapter of symmetrical lines; we intended to convey the idea that the lines in the back shall conform with those in the cushion, or vice versa. The way we arrive at the lines for the laying out of the plaits in the back and the cushion is as follows:

When starting to lay out our pattern, we mark on the seat board the exact center. Then we cover the back with the goods in the same way as we did with the cushion, marking around the blocking at bottom of back along the quarter lines; fitting closely along extreme edges at the top of the back. We then figure where to place the outer plait line, always allowing the outer block to be larger than the inner blocks. (Refer to page 67.) The pattern, as taken from the foundation, is laid on the bench and the drafting then takes place. We use the square, straight-edge and dividers, and space off from the outer lines, which have already been indicated, in suitable widths to meet the requirements.

Four to four and one-half inches is usually sufficient for the widths of the piping. The lines are drawn accurately, taking the bottom lines and the outer line for our objective points, working always from the center line that has been previously mentioned as marked on the center of the body and on the seat board. This plan is also followed in laying out the fullness pattern for the cushion. The spacing from the center of the back and cushion permits of accuracy, thus giving corresponding lines for the back and cushion.

The fullness pattern for the quarters is arrived at in the same manner. In order to construct the fullness pattern, the foundation patterns already having been described, a fitting thereof and the addition of the fullness required is necessary. This means simply an addition to the foundation pattern. For instance, if we are requiring a flat surface we would add five-eighths of one inch, or, if necessity requires it, three-quarters of one inch.

We mention this because of the fact that either a cotton filling may be required or a hair filling; but the average

BRUNN / Lincoln / WEM

amount of fullness, using the cotton filling, is five-eighths of one inch, thus allowing for one-quarter of one inch to be taken up by sewing on each plait and allowing three-eighths for filling. The fullness pattern is used for the cutting of the actual materials in which the job is to be trimmed.

In the cutting of materials, patterns should be made for all parts of the trimming, but we are using the above parts as a sample or demonstration. The fullness patterns are laid on the goods or material to be cut, which is cut out and punched to the exact size of the pattern. In cutting out, if leather is to be used, all the patterns which the size of the hide will permit should be laid on the hide before a single cut is made, so as to make sure there will be as little waste of material as possible. The exact lines of the pattern must be followed. Lines should be punched and drawn for sewing. This explanation is used only for jobs in custom shops and we are endeavoring to make it plain for the beginner. Where iarge production is required a different method would be used.

Having made the foundation patterns and the fullness patterns, and having the goods cut, it yet remains for us to sew the goods which have been cut from the fullness patterns to the foundation patterns. This is often done in custom shops by the trimmer himself, but in the larger shops experienced sewing machine operators are employed for this purpose. The sewing of the fullness must conform with that of the foundations which have been laid out, and must be strictly followed to secure harmonious lines.

The outer trimming having been sewed to the foundation, there yet remains the filling. The cotton filling is usually cut slightly less than the measurement of the foundation pattern. Three or four thicknesses of glazed cotton wadding, cotton batting of sufficient thickness or woven hair may be used. This is placed in position with a wooden paddle or pusher, the entire length required. Care should be taken that work is done smoothly. The outer covering of the French plait style of work is then ready to be placed in position.

BRUNN / Lincoln / WEM

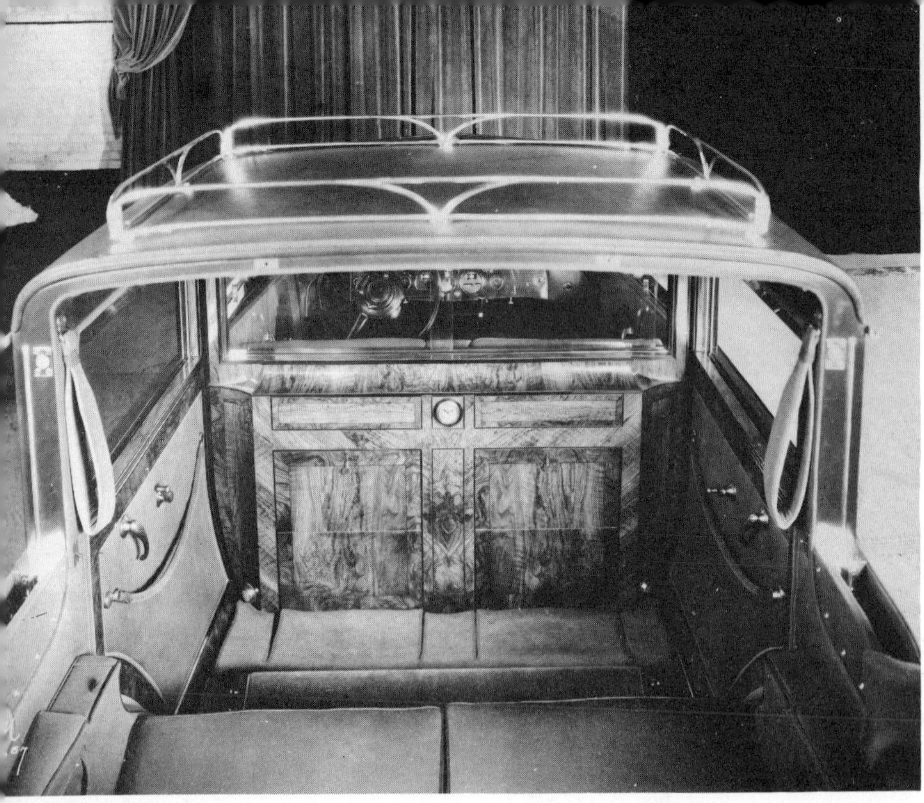

LOCKE / Duesenberg / CWM
LE BARON / Duesenberg / CWM

CHAPTER V

Covering Backs and Cushions

We will explain the covering of the back and cushion, which should suffice, as examples, for the other parts of the job.

In placing the outer covering on the cushion we must measure our foundation properly, find the exact measurement from the center to the outer line of plaits; start at the center; make outer lines conform both front and back, stretching smoothly and tightly front and back; tack to the wood frame of the cushion, underneath, stretching at the sides, causing the lines to become perfectly straight.

We fill in that space in the outer block with cotton or the other materials mentioned, to harmonize in thickness with the inner pipings already filled. Close in the sides in the same manner as the front and back, using the surplus goods at the corners to form a plait and "blind sew." Trim off the surplus material at the bottom, which has been tacked on the wood frame and the cushion is finished, with the exception of covering the bottom.

Ventilating holes must be provided in the bottom to the size of four inches in diameter; this is to give the cushion ventilation and to keep it from being air-bound. The seat board should also have an opening to permit the escape of compressed air, otherwise the effect of a comfortable cushion will be lost.

Hanging the Back

In this style of trimming (the French plait style) the back has been practically hung. It yet remains to place the outer covering. The outer covering being practically the same as that of the cushion, we hang the back, working from the center the same as on the cushion. We refer to our foundation pattern, get our measurements, and cause the lines to measure accordingly.

Working from the bottom and the top, the same measurements are followed, paying particular attention so that the pipe lines are straight.

Stretch tightly and smoothly, taking out all draws and wrinkles; turn in the surplus goods of the foundation around the sides of the spring and padding; fill in the outer block with the cotton or other fillings mentioned, in harmony with the inner pipings; throw the outer covering or leather into the corner around the spring and padding; close in entirely; tack smoothly at the top and bottom where the finish is required and trim off.

This is a simple method of doing the French plait style of work, causing the lines of the back and cushion to be in harmony with each other, for it is essential on first-class work that this harmony be secured.

One-Piece Trimming Door to Door

A discussion has sometimes arisen among trimmers as to whether the French plait style of trimming on a rear or front back, running from door to door, could be made in one section. It can. And to do it is a comparatively simple operation.

The back and quarters are made in separate sections, exactly the same as if we were making the back and quarters separately. These parts, after being made up, are tacked in the job over the padding temporarily, after the pipes have been filled as in the ordinary manner. They are then placed in position, fitted, marked out exactly in the same manner as we would fit a slip cover, and are sewed together at the corners (on the machine), which represents a continuation of the piping.

Where sewed together at the corner the four blocks, or the two corner blocks on each side, being triangular in shape, could not very handily be filled with the cotton or filling used for the piping, but as the backs are being hung permanently over the covering or foundation pads, these corner pipes referred to should be filled with hair, presenting the same appearance as if the entire back was fitted and laid out in one piece.

Top Making

Any consideration of top making should always be with reference to the type of car for which the top is intended. Various styles of bodies require different overhang at the rear bow. The position in which the windshield is set regulates the length of the top.

Bow manufacturers who make a specialty of furnishing different types of patented tops furnish the body builder with a drawing for the ordering of bows suitable for the style of car for which they are intended. These may be followed with more or less satisfaction, but certain rules must be adopted in order that a satisfactorily shaped top may be produced, or, in other words, a top too high or a top too low would spoil the appearance of a well-designed body.

Setting Bows and Trimming the Top

It has been found from actual experience that the average measurement from the floor boards to the main bow should not exceed 52 inches, nor should it be less than 50 inches. The overhang of the rear bow varies as to the construction of the rear panel, varying from no overhang or nothing to 2½ inches.

The front bow should project sufficiently over the windshield to permit a proper appearance, also taking into consideration the kind of windshield fasteners to be used.

The drop of the front bow below the main bow should average 5 inches. The drop of the rear bow should average 3 inches. The second bow and fourth bow should be on a line from the first to the third bow, and the third bow to the fifth bow, on a five-bow top.

The width is arrived at according to the construction of the job, measuring the width at the goosenecks and causing the bow holders or saddles to be placed in the position in which the top when thrown will fall free.

So much for the "setting" of the top; now for the "trimming." Various kinds of top materials may be used, such as mohair, cotton goods, substitute leathers and rubberized materials.

Method of Trimming a Top

Many different styles of tops are now in use. Some are "freakish," but we are going to treat of a conservative style of top and its trimming.

The bows being set in position on the job, we must hold them in position by means of a temporary strainer over the top, and from the top of the back bow to the body. The wood part of the bows, or the top of them, is covered with a light material to match the goods of the top. The permanent strainers are then tacked in their respective places; quarter pads are made of the same material, stretched and tacked in position. These quarter pads should be on an average of 8 inches in width, running the entire length of the top. The padding or filling is placed therein, and either cotton or hair may be used for the padding. The padding is then permanently closed by sewing. Some paste the upper covering of the pad, but this method is no longer approved by good practice.

Pads and strainers being placed in position, goods for the deck, quarters, back curtains and side curtains are cut. We usually fit the quarters first by stretching them over the pad, marking out the quarters for the position in which they are intended to be placed when finished.

The next thing to do is to stretch the deck into position, extending over the quarters; turned under along the quarter line intended; creased down and marked, marking the quarters and deck along the quarter line at one time, scoring marks with chalk by which the operator can follow with the stitching of the seam.

Back curtains may be made in various shapes and styles, but the fact should be emphasized that in custom work the fitting of all parts must be done separately in order to insure a perfect job. The top and back curtains being fitted, the finish of the edges varies. On some tops there is a round

ROLLSTON / Duesenberg / CWM
ROLLSTON / Duesenberg JN / CWM

binding finish; on others a straddle binding. Very often it is just hemmed and trimmed off.

Care should be taken that the bows are perfectly in line. Care should also be taken in drawing on the top and placing the back curtain in position that a natural strain be given the goods, otherwise, when thrown and being placed back in its original position, the top will be under a severe strain, owing to the fact that the material has been stretched too tight.

There are usually six side curtains for a large car, and these should be fitted as a unit and marked off at the same time to get a perfect fitting, owing to the fact that on custom jobs there is variation.

The fitting of a well-made boot is quite an effort and the fitting should be done on the individual car. It should not be too tight nor too full, and should be fitted when the top is completed. The matter of cutting varies according to the size of the top.

Some Incentives to Good Work

The demand for luxury in automobile bodies, and the consequent striving on the part of manufacturers to excel each other have constituted the motives behind the modern development of automobile upholstery work to the plane of genuine art.

The designer of automobile upholstery today must be an artist if he expects more than a moderate degree of success. He must be a close student, a diligent and watchful observer. His faculty for the proper blending of lines and colors must be well developed and a full appreciation of the value of harmony must be one of his most important qualifications.

The above observation applies just as strongly to the designer in a factory turning out hundreds of cars as to the designer in a custom shop, even though the responsibility is of such a different character. The factory designer, whose production is large, whose costs must be maintained at a minimum, and whose styles must appeal to the multitude, has a big proposition to face. His ideas may be good, the execution may be well performed, yet costs of production may make his design prohibitive.

On the other hand, the cost of production may be within bounds, yet it may not appeal to the public, which would be a most serious condition and hamper sales. The responsibility attached to the proper designing of upholstery may therefore be realized.

The custom designer, however, has a different proposition. Usually the customer believes he knows what he wants; he selects his materials and suggests the style of trimming to be used, pointing out particular features he wants emphasized.

Individual vs. Quantity Production

The big difference in the two types of upholstering lies in the fact that the factory production must appeal to the general buying public, while the custom-made body must satisfy in all details the individual buying it. For that reason, in a custom-built body, greater stress is laid on upholstering and its details than in a factory job.

The factory job is sold with the chassis as a unit—a factory product—and while it is expected to render service, it is never subjected to the critical inspection or called upon to render the service expected of a custom-built body.

The car built in quantities, which is sold as a unit, must of necessity have appealing lines, a body of utility, pleasing and comfortable upholstery, but it is often upon the satisfaction which the engine renders that continued sales can be based. The body, if there is beauty in its lines, and the upholstery, if comfortable and well made, add greatly in making sales easier.

On the other hand, the custom-built job must rely solely upon the service and satisfaction which the body, its upholstery, etc., render. The body alone is responsible for continued patronage. It can therefore be easily realized that the methods used in upholstering a custom-built job are totally different from those of factory production.

Renault / SMacM

CHAPTER VI

Tufted Work and Its Characteristics

It is our purpose in this chapter to treat of tufted work, and we think it well to call attention at this point to various features, both good and bad, which are characteristic of this type of work, particularly the diamond or half diamond style. It is first of all harder to lay out, harder to execute, requires more material and is more difficult to keep clean, but, on the other hand, permits a greater display of skill, has longer life, is more comfortable, and is, by most people, thought more beautiful.

The reason for diamond tufted work requiring more material lies in the fact that considerably more fullness is used, varying from one-half inch to one inch more than in the French plait style. This amount of fullness, multiplied by the number of pipes, represents considerable material.

These remarks, of course, apply only to the upholstering materials, because the foundations would be almost identical in the amount of goods required.

Diamond Tufted Work

The laying out of diamond tufted work should be adapted to the particular type of car for which it is intended. In the large, roomy limousine there would be permitted a greater amount of fullness than could be used in a smaller type of car. In the cases mentioned the experience of the trimmer has taught him the amount of fullness necessary.

The calculation for fullness varies in cloth and leather. Cloth has more stretch, and often we use slightly less fullness than we would were we using leather. Fullness required also varies according to the size of the diamond.

A large diamond requires less fullness in proportion than the smaller diamonds. The smaller diamond holds up better after use than does the large diamond, for the reason that a lesser degree of shifting of the hair is permitted in the small diamond, while the larger diamond has the advantage probably of being softer. But these variations are overcome, to a certain extent, by expert workmanship. Some trimmers prefer a diamond not to exceed in size six and one-half inches long and proportionate in width.

There are certain methods to be followed in the laying out of diamond tufted work that are essential to follow. These rules being followed, there will be but little cause for complaint.

In laying out the work, the requirements of the employer are considered from an economic standpoint. The more fullness required the more material used. Large output considered, the matter of fullness amounts to a considerable sum in materials used, either cloth, leather, hair or cotton.

Fullness required varies from three-quarters inch to one and one-half inches; on factory outputs three-quarters inch is used; on custom work one inch appears to be about the average. Where three-quarters inch fullness is used in the width of the diamond three-eighths inch would be the amount to use in the length of the diamond. When in doubt as to the proper amount of fullness to use in length we would suggest this simple method in order to find the correct amount of fullness:

Fullness Allowances in Tufted Work

Fullness across the diamond is determined by instruction from the employer, or, if left to the trimmer, according to the requirements of the job.

For the purpose of explanation, we will say that one inch has been decided upon for fullness across the diamond. Now it is necessary for us to know exactly what fullness is required in length, which we can easily determine in this manner:

Take a piece of string one inch longer than the width of the diamond; tack on the points as laid out on the foundation pattern for the width of the diamond; raise it into a position describing an arc; tack another piece of string at

A Closed Car Interior, Showing a Good Example of Tufted or "Biscuit" Style Upholstery.

the point forming the end of the length of the diamond; raise this piece of string into a position describing an arc the same height as that across the diamond and mark the length of the string required to reach the other end of the length of the diamond.

The difference between the length of this piece of string and the distance between the two points representing the length of the diamond is the fullness required. This is a very simple method and insures absolute smoothness.

The fullness may be calculated accurately by one thoroughly versed in higher mathematics, but since it is seldom that trimmers have been fortunate enough to have had the advantage of this training, the above simple, practical and accurate method will be found easy and reliable.

Making Pattern for Cushion and Laying Out Pattern for Diamond Tufting

The spring being ready, we will take a piece of duck of sufficient size to cover the entire cushion, that is to say the top and the four sides. The spring we are using has been attached to the wood frame at the bottom, which is now generally used. Tack the goods, entirely covering the spring, to the wood frame temporarily, and mark around the outer spring edge and the bottom of the wood frame.

After the material is so marked remove the goods; lay it on the bench smoothly; draw positive lines which represent the spring edge at the top and the wood frame at the bottom, striking a line about three inches in from the spring edge all around the top. From this line we arrive at our objective lines for the laying out of the diamonds. Our dividers are then used for the spacing of the width of the diamonds.

The finding of the width of the diamond is arrived at in the following manner:

Sometimes a diamond and one-half pattern is used, sometimes two diamonds or two and one-half diamonds.

Having divided the distance between the objective lines at the front and back of the pattern, using the rule that the width of the diamond must be more than one-half and less than two-thirds of the length, we can readily arrive at an approximate figure for the width of the diamond.

BRUNN / Lincoln / WEM

For an example, we will say that the length of the diamond is nine inches; one-half of nine is four and one-half, and two-thirds of nine is six; so that the width of our diamond must be more than four and one-half inches and less than six inches. Taking any figure between these two, say five inches, we divide five into the distance between our objective lines at the sides of our pattern, which will give us equal spaces and a half of a space, which would be unsightly.

We can easily see that the width should be slightly less than five inches, equally divided, so we will divide the distance between our objective line at the sides into equal spaces. Thus we arrive at the width required.

The Diamond and Half Diamond

In order to complete the pattern for the diamond and half diamond, after objective lines are laid out and spacing is done, for the width of the pattern for these points we will strike three equal points across the width of the cushion, marking from the second line to the fourth or rear objective line, which gives the length of the diamond.

Mark diagonally from the outside tufts on the second line to the second tuft on the rear or fourth line. Continue to mark diagonally across the pattern; reverse and mark the opposite way across the pattern. This completes the diamond inside the objective lines.

Then draw lines from the outer line of tufts square to the outer edges, thus completing the lines for the foundation pattern. Where a cord is sewed in the cushion around the top, three-eighths of one inch should be allowed over the size of the spring.

Layout of the Two-Diamond Style

For the two-diamond layout the outside objective lines are in the same position, but we divide the width of the cushion into four equal parts and the pattern is made in the same manner as the diamond and one-half design, with this

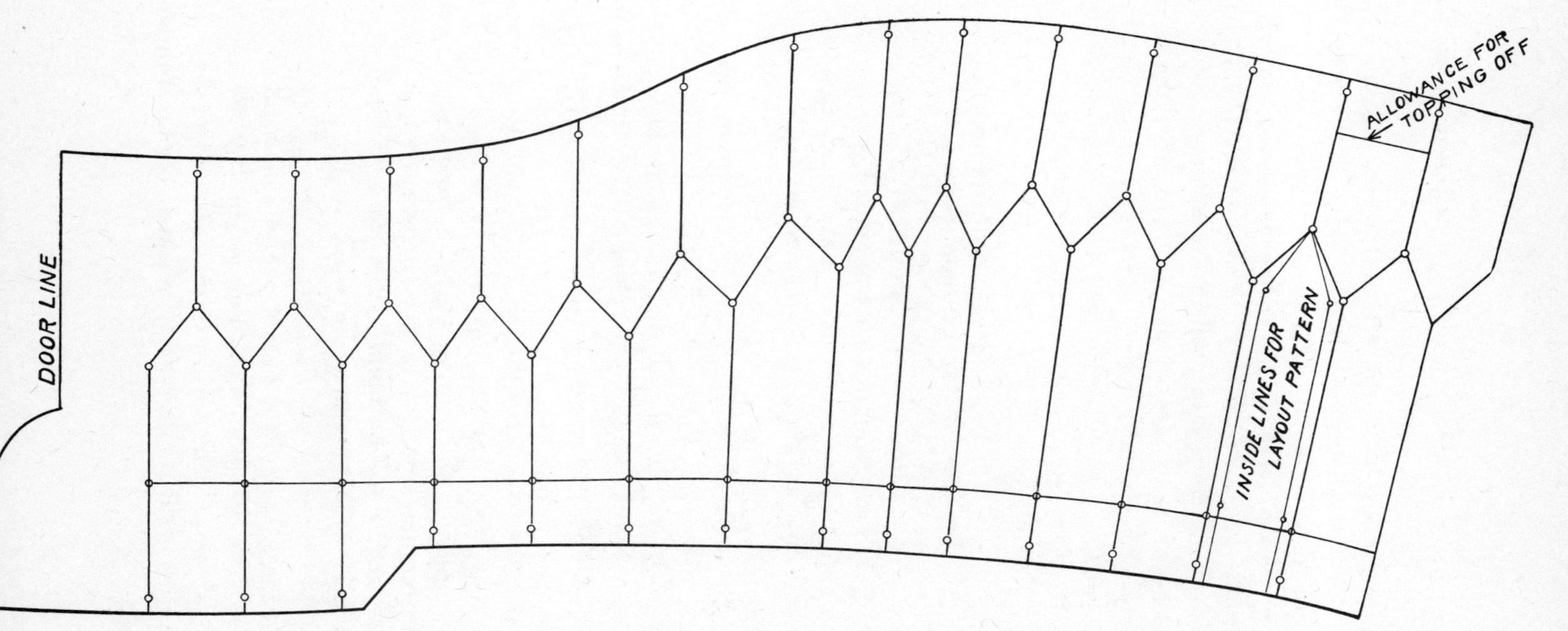

ONE-HALF FULLNESS PATTERN FOR FIVE-PASSENGER TOURING CAR.
Showing Lines for Layout and Fullness Patterns and Allowance for Topping Off.

difference, that we lay out for the width of the diamond from the second and fourth lines. The fullness pattern is made in exactly the same manner as if laying out the foundation pattern, with the addition of the fullness required.

While we have allowed a certain amount of fullness, we have taken into consideration the sewing, which consumes about one-quarter of one inch of the fullness. The sewing is done on all the lines indicated in the pattern.

The best way is to sew all the way out from the outer line of tufts, thus permitting the lines as laid out to be followed absolutely. In the sewing it is well to jump a stitch or two each side of the tuft, as this permits of all the fullness and allows the tuft to sink in deeper.

Making Up the Cushion Top

In making up the top a wood frame of sufficient size is covered with a duck suitable for top making, on which is laid the foundation patterns which have been described. The tufts and lines are then marked from the pattern on the frame.

Hair in a sufficient quantity is laid on the frame, the lines as marked giving the shape to which the hair is laid, of sufficient height to round out the fullness required. The experienced trimmer knows about the height required for the different fullnesses.

Over the hair is placed a layer of cotton. We might mention here the reason for the use of cotton. Cotton prevents the hair from working through the cloth, if cloth is used. We might also mention that the trimmer in laying hair, picks the hair apart or loosens it, which requires considerable time if done by hand. Well-equipped shops use a hair picker, which permits the work to be done more rapidly.

The outside covering is then laid over the hair and cotton, and fastened to the foundation temporarily by the use of upholsterers' pins. The tufts are then drawn through the outer covering to the tuft marks indicated on the foundation. The tufts are tightened to a backing of cord or rolled strips of muslin, drawn tightly by means of a slip knot, which is tied securely.

After the tufts are all drawn in position the plaits are turned and regulated. On first-class work care is taken that the plaits are all turned the one way, to the left. The reason we turn the plaits to the left is that brushing or cleaning is usually done working from the right to the left; thus we avoid forcing the plaits out of position.

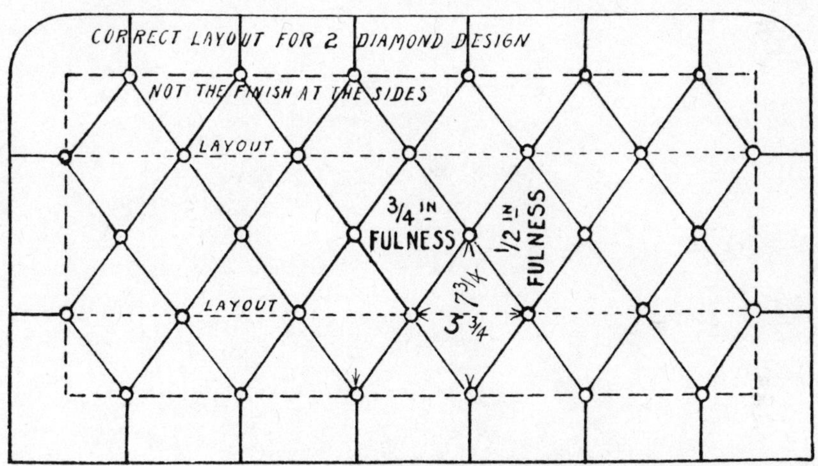

Correct Layout for Two-Diamond Design.

The tufts being in position permanently, we must see that the diamonds are perfectly smooth. Very often we must work the hair up to the buttons by the use of a stuffing rod and regulator.

The inside of the cushion top being completed, we begin to draw from the outer line of tufts to the sewing line of the cord, if a corded top is to be used. We stretch out smoothly at the lines indicated, shifting the upholsterers' pins, taking up the fullness at each plait, drawing smoothly between the plaits at the outer lines and sewing through all around the outer line of the cushion, indicating the cord line.

Where the corded top is used a facing is necessary. The facing pattern is obtained by fitting around the cushion

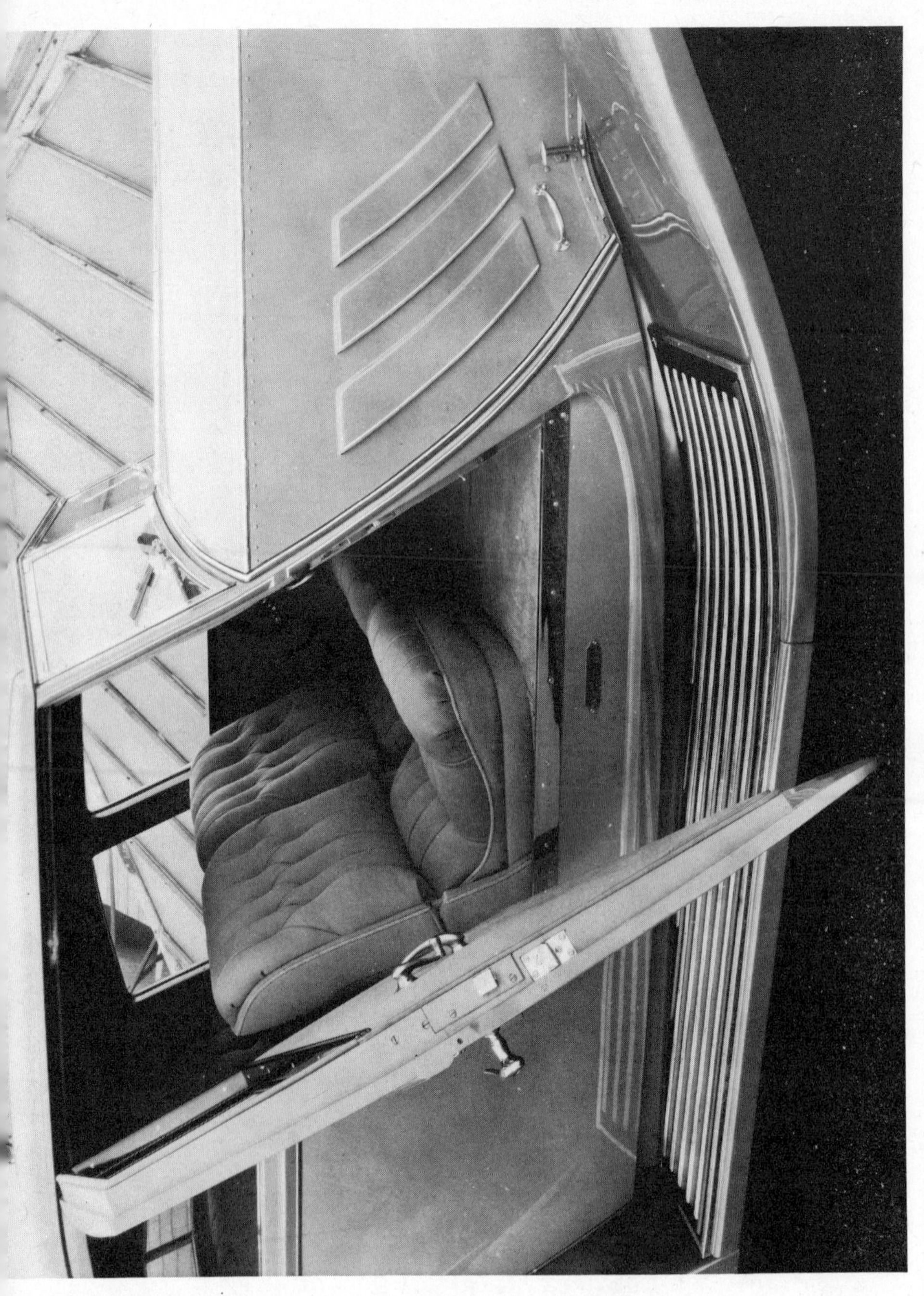

BREWSTER / Rolls-Royce P II / SMacM

spring, marking off the upper part of the spring edge and the bottom part of the wood frame of the cushion.

The goods being cut to the pattern, a cord is sewed around the top part of the goods, a sufficient amount being allowed for the "take-up" of the cord, which is usually about three-eighths of one inch. The facing is then sewed around the cushion top while on the frame.

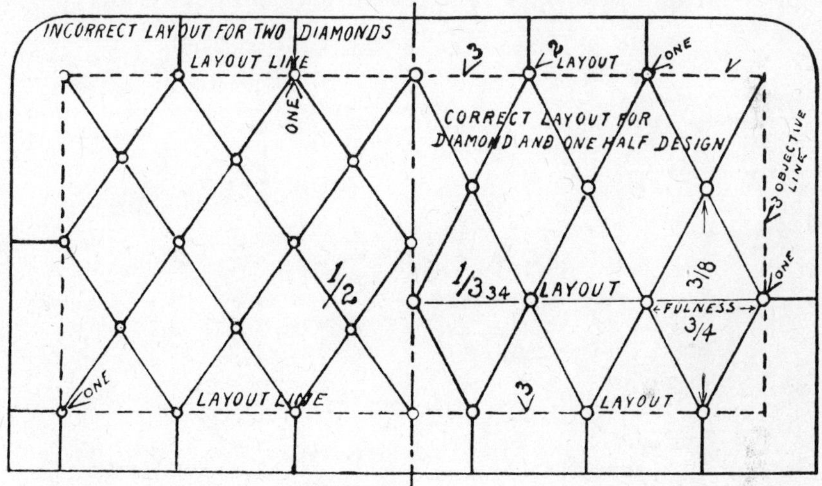

Incorrect Layout for Two Diamonds.

Correct Layout for Diamond and Half Diamond Design.

Attaching Top to the Spring

Let us now attach the top to the spring in this manner: Either the sides of the spring are covered with suitable goods or the top and sides are covered and tacked to the wood frame. The top, which has been made, is sewed fast to this sub-foundation, either around the spring edge or underneath it, but the sub-foundation should be whipped (whip stitched) to the top of the spring, thus avoiding the shifting of the top when sewed into position. The facing is then drawn down and nailed to the underneath part of the bottom of the spring or wood frame. The bottom is then closed in with a covering of canvas or enameled duck.

Providing Good Ventilation

Ventilation should be provided in all cushions by means of grommets on the sides and rear facings, together with ventilating holes in the bottom. A cushion, to give satisfactory results, must be well ventilated, otherwise the compressed air will cause unsatisfactory results in an otherwise perfect cushion. It should be mentioned here that the use of good hair is always required to give proper results.

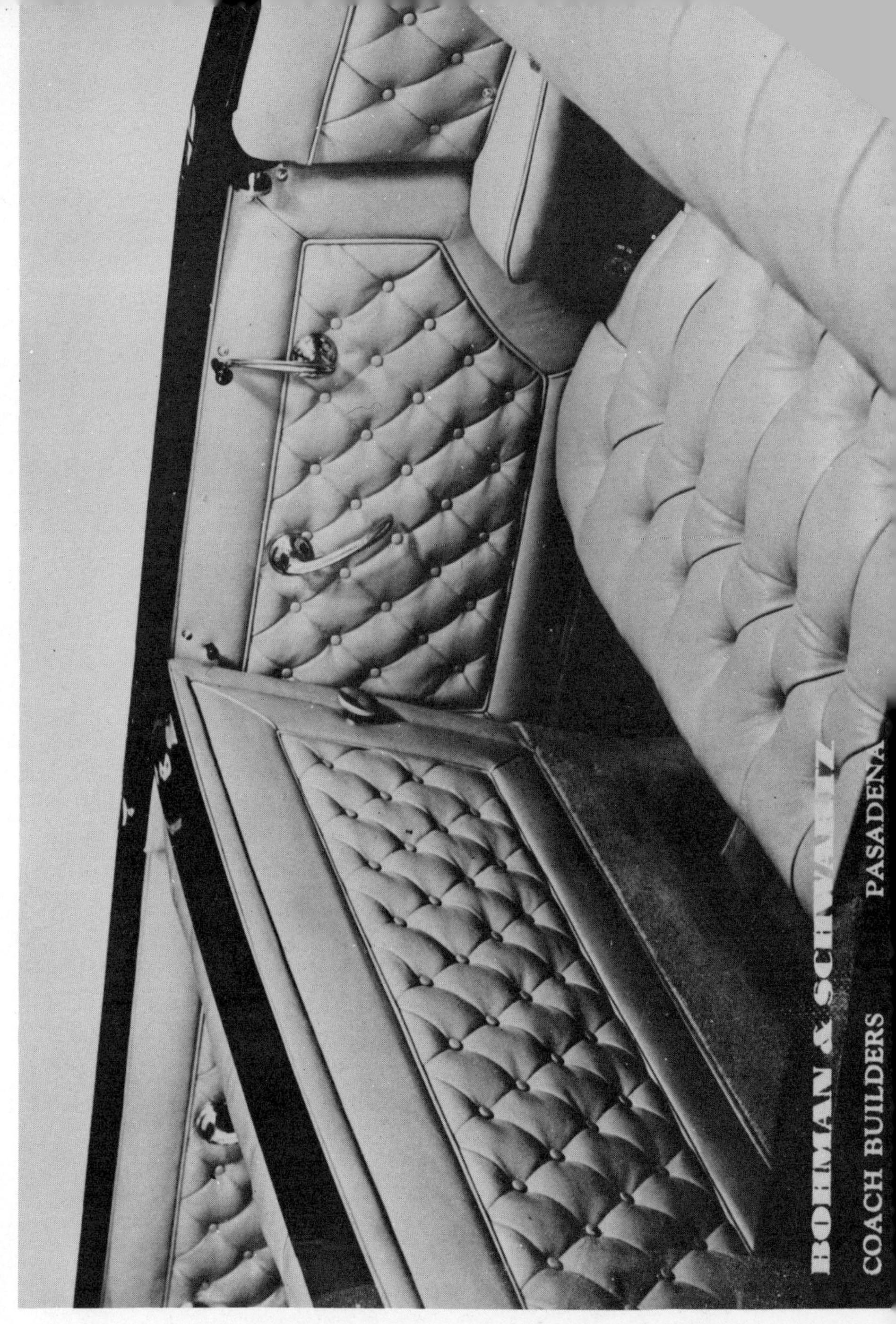

BOHMAN & SCHWARTZ / Duesenberg / CWM

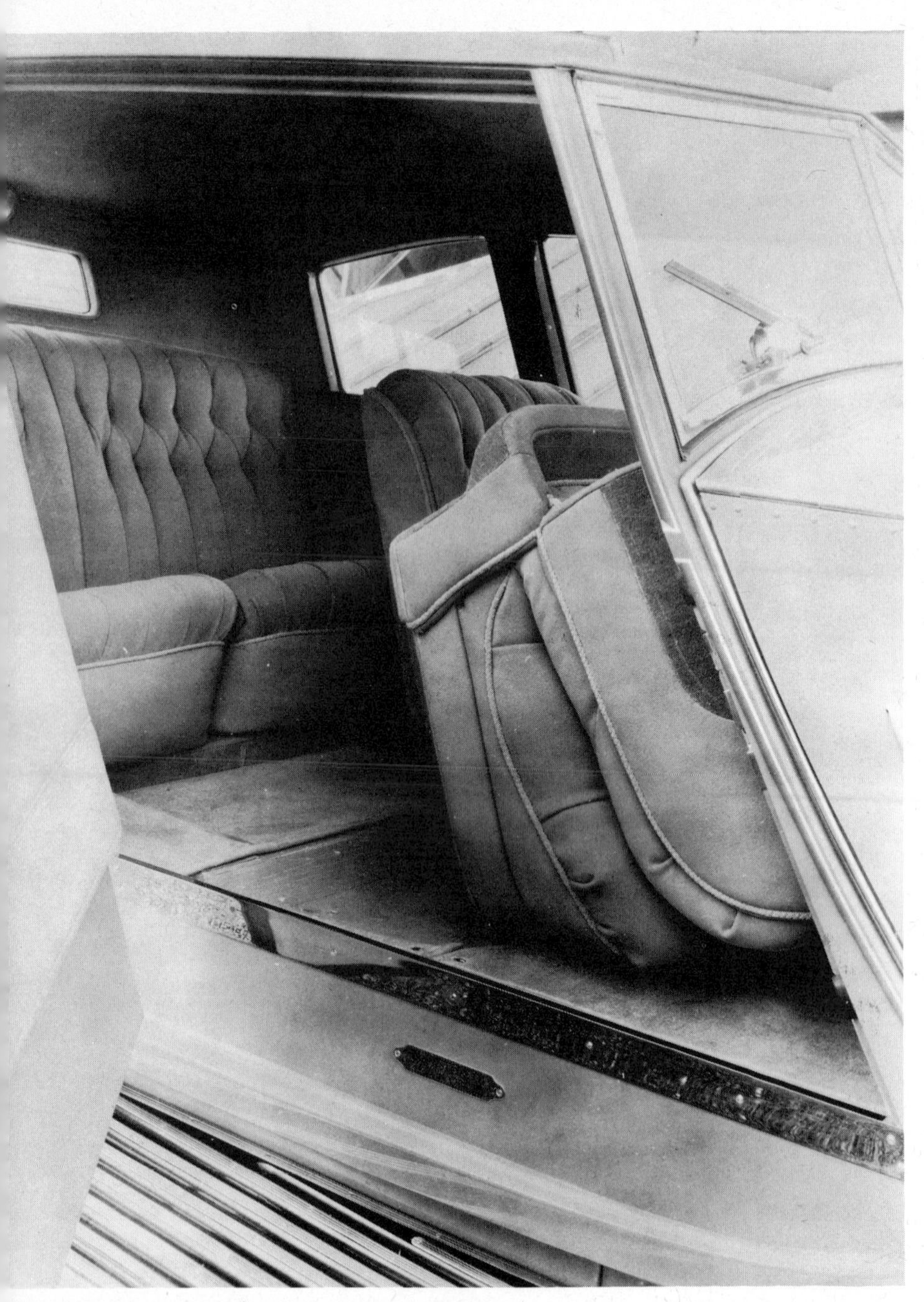

BREWSTER / Rolls-Royce PII / SMacM

CHAPTER VII

Laying Out and Making Up a Diamond Seat Back

Fitting the pattern for the back is done in two ways—either by fitting over the springs or simply to the frame. Fitting over the springs probably would be the better method for custom work, but allowances can be made without the use of the spring.

The average amount of "take-up" is about two and one-half inches, so if a pattern is made or fitted to the frame this amount of allowance should be made for the "take-up" of the spring.

The material from which the pattern is to be made is tacked temporarily over the spring construction; the outer lines where the finish is required is marked while in position, at top, bottom and sides, allowance being made on the sides for the thickness of the quarters.

Calculation is then made for the outer line of piping, which is determined from the bottom. The average position for this point is about four inches from the center of the radius at the seat board. Thus we have found our objectives, which are (1) the top finish, (2) the seat board where the back comes in contact with the quarter, and (3) the outer line of piping.

The pattern is then removed, the center is marked, and the dividing of the width of the pipes from the outer line gives the width of the pipings. We should work at all times from the center in laying out the foundation for both the back and cushion.

In diamond tufting, the first row of buttons should average five inches from the top. From the top line of tufts to the point of the diamond should average three and one-half inches, and the bottom lines of tufts should be placed about three inches above the top of the finished cushion.

The fullness required across the back varies as in the cushion, one inch being the average. The fullness between the points at the top of the back averages three-eighths of one inch. Fullness from the points to the bottom line of tufts varies according to the contour required, from one-quarter of one inch for a flat back to one and three-quarter inches for a full back.

The fullness pattern is determined in the same manner as the foundation pattern, being an exact duplicate, with the addition of the fullness required, and the amount of goods required for a turn-under at the side and a finish for top and bottom.

The patterns for back diamond tufting, when completed, are made up on a frame in exactly the same manner as the cushion top, with the difference that the top and bottom are left open, and are closed in with the hanging of the back.

In laying out of both the back and the cushion we are working always from the center lines, working to the center in the hanging of the back and the building of the cushion, following closely the lines of the foundation patterns.

In the hanging of the back the center is marked on the seat board; the foundation pattern is measured to ascertain the distance between the outer lines for the piping, which is marked on the seat, and the lines of the back are caused to conform with these measurements when hanging the back. The same method is pursued in the building of the cushion, thus causing all the plaits to conform.

It is the purpose in this book only to give methods, descriptions and examples, without the complete trimming of any particular or individual job, taking only into consideration that these instructions are intended primarily for beginners in the art of automobile upholstery.

The Different Varieties of "Diamond" Tufting

There being various styles in which diamond tufting can be used, we will submit drawings showing the half-diamond pipe back and a full-diamond pipe back, a back made separately with separate side quarters and a one-piece back running from door to door. In making the one-piece back we will call attention to the proper method of making the pattern.

Owing to the fact that in a one-piece back the lines are drawn absolutely square, there will be a tendency to have the appearance of the line not being squared up. This is an optical illusion. While the lines will appear to be out of plumb, it is caused by the contour made by the springs. So to overcome this optical illusion, while laying out our pattern, we contract the outer line marked inside the radius of the seat at the bottom, three-eighths of one inch for the first line, one-quarter for the second line, one-eighth for the third line, the rest of the lines for the pipes to the center being square up. This will make the lines appear absolutely square.

This method being followed in the laying out of the back pattern in one piece will permit of easy back hanging, especially where many jobs are being built for an order. For large output the first pattern as it is laid out may not be absolutely correct, but while the first back is being hung deductions can be made, the pattern can be altered and will suffice for an indefinite number of jobs.

On large outputs particular attention should be paid to the amount of wastage. This should also be deducted from the original pattern. We are calling attention to this fact as an economic example, for an inch wasted here and there is not an economical proposition. The beginner should bear in mind these facts, for a dollar saved by the firm which employs him means a more stable position for himself as well as securing credit for his own efforts.

It has often been questioned, "is a one-piece back and quarters as comfortable as one made in three sections?" What we have learned from experience is that there is as much comfort and satisfaction in a one-piece construction as in a three-piece construction. So far as comfort is concerned there is no difference.

On a one-piece back running from door to door, the

radius at the corners will be maintained permanently, while on a back made in three sections, viz., back proper and side quarters, being free at the corners, has a tendency to sink in and become square and lose the radius altogether, causing a hollow to be made to which the body will not conform.

We mention the above as an example, for the reason that invariably a person riding in a car will endeavor to seat himself comfortably in the corner, and after all fair deductions are made, even after taking into consideration that a one-piece back may be air-bound, we still find that the one-piece back has the advantage, because outlets for the air can be provided by the use of grommets below the top line of the cushion, these grommets, of course, being concealed from view.

Sensible Spring Construction

Much of the success attributed to a trimmer as to comfort depends on proper spring construction. The utmost care should be taken to have properly fitted springs of the right construction. There have been many patented springs placed upon the market, and these have given more or less satisfaction. Freak spring construction is seldom satisfactory, either to the maker of the car or the user.

The height of the spring determines the gauge of the wire to be used in making the spring. The spring must have a sufficient resistance to take the bound and rebound and yet be resilient enough to permit of comfortable riding. The day is past for a trimmer to create his own spring construction and he is relieved of this effort by the seat spring manufacturer.

In fitting spring patterns, care should be taken that the spring does not bind, either at the back or quarters, and it should have a pitch or an incline toward the rear, on the cushion spring. The average pitch required in present-day construction is three inches. The reason for having the pitch is to incline the rider toward the back, and the back spring should rake toward the top. This combination in spring construction permits of the utmost comfort.

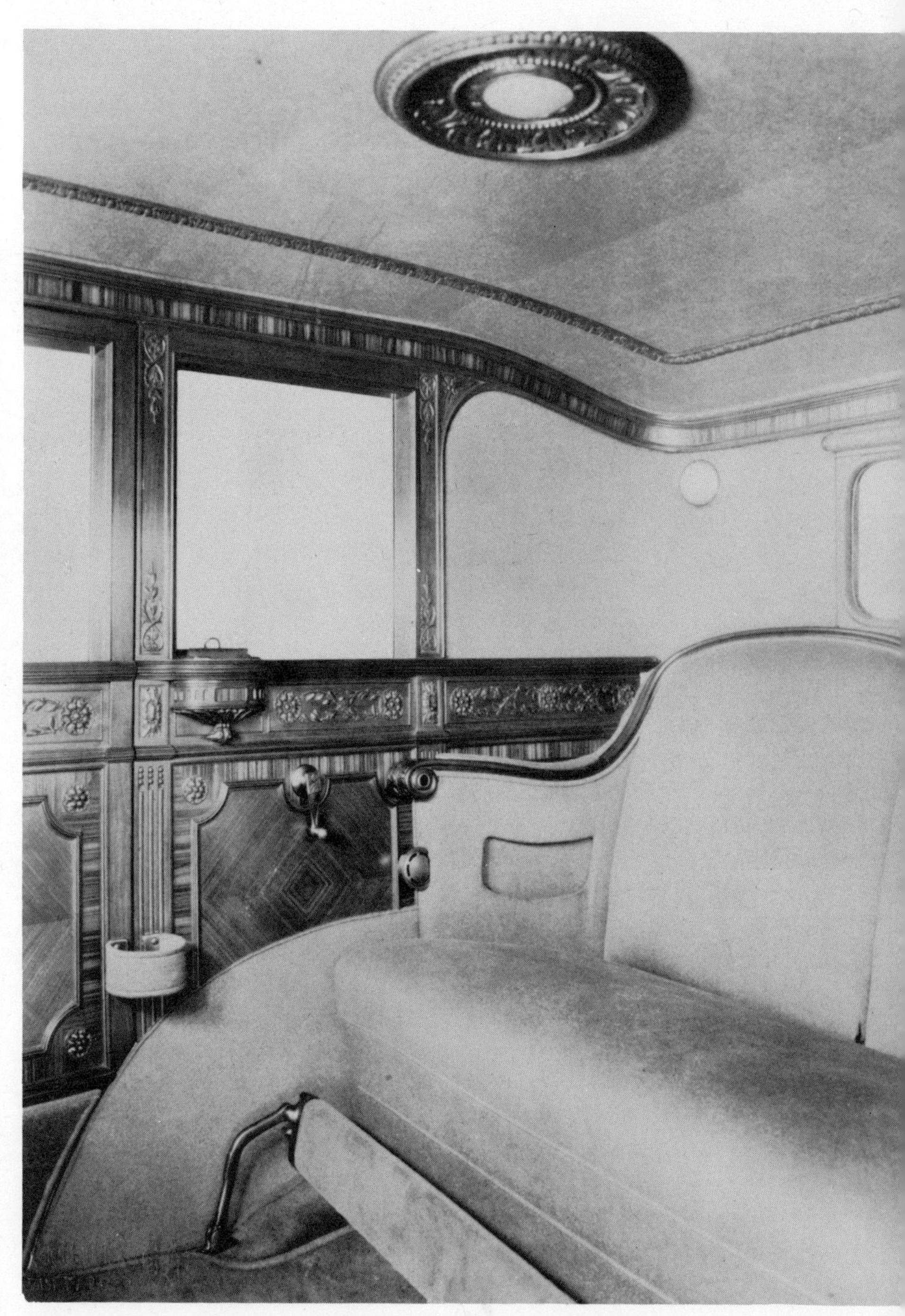

BRUNN / Lincoln / MMcC

The use of too much hair, or making the back pad of the cushion pad too thick, drawing down the cushion too tight or hanging the back too tight, will cause the springs to lose their effect, making them stiff. The springs should always have their full freedom so that the maximum of results may be attained. Back spring construction is so made that there is no shifting permitted, and no tying in of springs is done. This condition permits of rapid back hanging.

CHAPTER VIII

The Negligee and Plain Styles

Negligee work, which is considered by many people the finest, most beautiful and most comfortable upholstery, is today almost entirely unknown to the majority of mechanics. The beauty of this style lies in the fact of its apparent looseness, the graceful and natural folds of the goods showing the application of real mechanical skill.

The laying out of patterns for negligee work is done practically in the same manner as the diamond tufted work, but with this difference: There is no plaiting, fullness need not exceed three-eighths of one inch, and the diamonds are made considerably smaller. Cushion tops are made almost invariably with a corded edge and plain facings.

In order to get the extreme effect in negligee work it is necessary that the cloth should be lined with a layer of cotton wadding and muslin. The cloth, after being cut out, is laid on the bench, back up; the punch marks for the buttons are touched lightly with paste over which a layer of cotton is placed. The outer edges of the cloth are also pasted just beyond where the cord is intended to be sewed. The cotton is trimmed off just inside this, pasting at the outer edges, and the muslin backing is laid over the cotton.

Care should be taken that none of the three pieces of material is stretched, thereby allowing each section to have an equal amount of fullness, so that when the tufting is done each piece of material has an equal amount of play. This section is then laid aside for the paste to dry.

The foundation pattern is laid on the covered frame, which is marked to correspond with the foundation pattern. Two layers of hair are laid on the frame and the outer covering laid over the hair, held temporarily in place by the use of upholsterers' pins. The buttons or tufts are pulled through at the points indicated on the pattern, drawn very tightly, tied fast and with the use of a tickler creates an indentation along the lines from button to button. This causes the impression of a line between the diamonds.

Pat lightly with the hands all over the top, thus flattening out the hair. Use a regulator through the back to work the hair up to the button. Very often it is required to use a stuffing rod in order to fill up any hollow that may be caused by the shifting of the hair while working up the pad.

After this has been done draw the outer line of plaits firmly to the outer edges where the cord finish is to be placed. The goods between the outer lines is to be left natural and the sewing is done by hand around the cord line, sewing the cloth to the frame covering.

The stitching is done the same as a basting stitch, up and down, in spaces of about one-half inch, not back stitched under any consideration. The up and down stitch causes an indentation which gives the negligee effect. The back stitch would cause the appearance of a series of small plaits, and this we must avoid, otherwise we would not create the negligee effect.

No creasing or ironing is required, for in order to get the negligee effect there must be no plaits formed, and the material must find its natural position to create the desired negligee effect.

The advantage of negligee work is that after use it usually improves in appearance, proving that the goods must find a natural position in the make-up. Negligee work properly executed is very attractive and serviceable, and always excites admiration.

After the top is sewed in the above manner the facing, with a cord attached, is sewed by hand around the lines which have been basted. The sewing should be done by the well-known trimmer's back stitch. The back stitch adds more strength and will not affect at this point the negligee effect.

BRUNN / Lincoln / WEM

In making up the back the outer covering is made in the same manner as described for the cushion top, but in making up the back foundation a pad is required before the outer covering is placed in position.

We will now describe the method of making this back on the frame, as all negligee work is frame work. The frame being covered, the pattern is marked thereon; a pad about two inches thick is made of sufficient size as indicated in drawing. The pad should be made extending a couple of inches beyond the point where the buttons are to be placed, that is, top and sides. At the bottom of the back the pad should finish a half inch above the bottom line of buttons. The pad should be flat and loosely quilted through, thus keeping the hair permanently in position. Over the pad is piled hair the size of the pad; over the hair is placed the outer covering.

The buttons are drawn through, and care should be taken that the buttons are drawn perpendicular to the marks indicated for the buttons on the foundation, because if the buttons are not drawn through the pad properly there will be a variation in the fullness.

The two top lines of tufts are drawn down just as far as the pad. The bottom line of buttons, as already indicated, are to be placed below the pad, which allows the bottom line of buttons to set deeper than the upper line, thus giving a square effect and causing a back to be made that will hold its original shape indefinitely.

The buttons being tied securely in position, we will finish the sides and the bottom. The body of the back having the lines regulated into position and the hair worked up smoothly, the bottom is drawn down to the finish line and basted.

No hair is required from the bottom line of tufts to the bottom finish, thus permitting this section at the bottom to be flat, which allows the cushion to extend under the "belly" of the back, permitting more cushion room and giving the benefit of the maximum space.

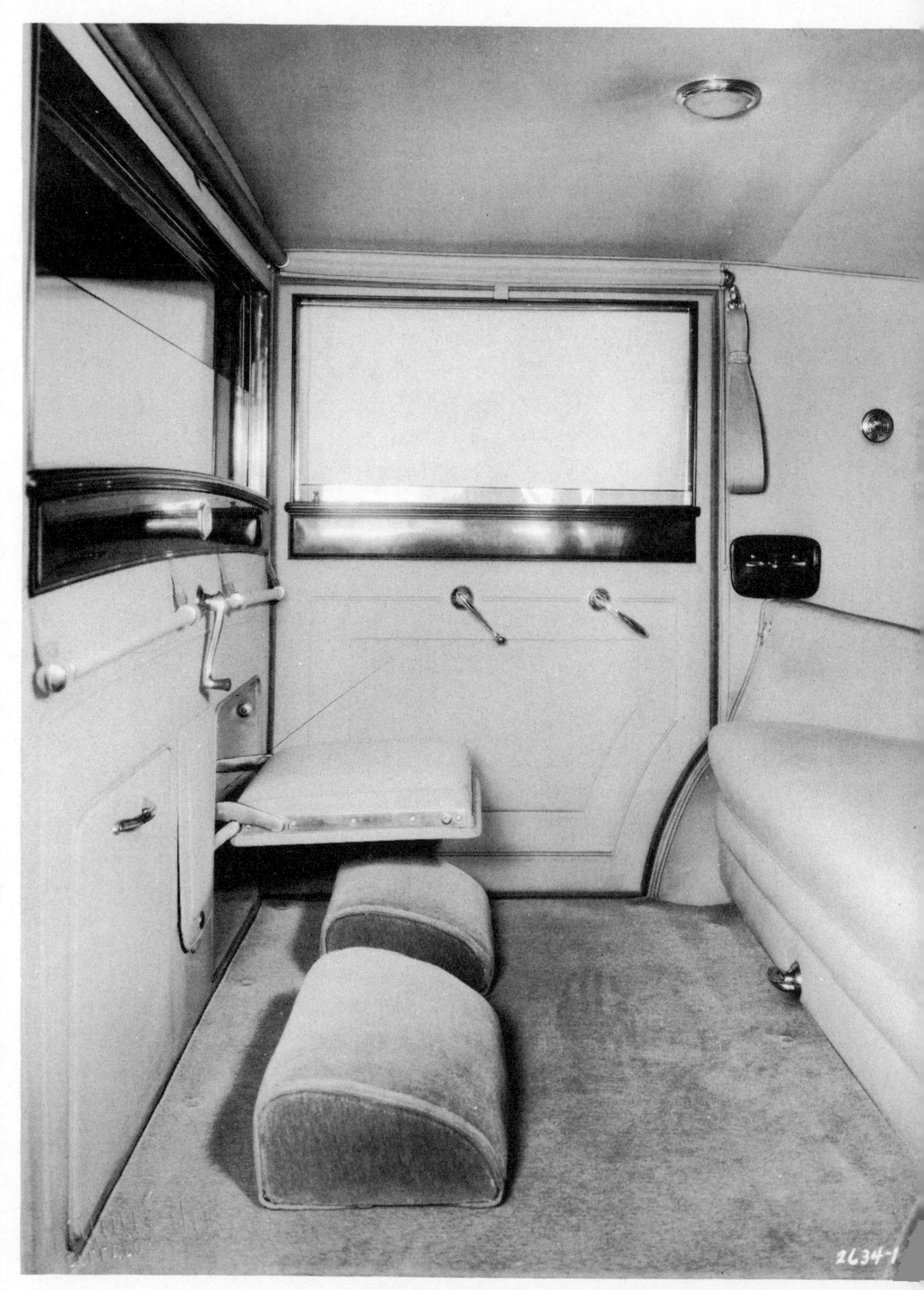

BRUNN / *Lincoln* / WEM

That section of the side between the pad and the quarter line is filled in with hair and the cloth is basted down at the quarter line, indicated from the top to the bottom. The foundation is cut from top to bottom and the surplus cloth is thrown around and basted to the rear of the back.

The top of the back can be finished in the same way as the bottom by basting in position, or it can be left open and closed in when hanging the back in the job, but often the closing in on the frame can be accomplished with less effort and requires much less time in hanging.

The making of the quarters can be done either on a frame at the bench or it can be made up on double-ply buckram as a foundation and can be finished in the job. The fullness can be worked in by the tacking at the finish edges. The above description is for separate backs and quarters.

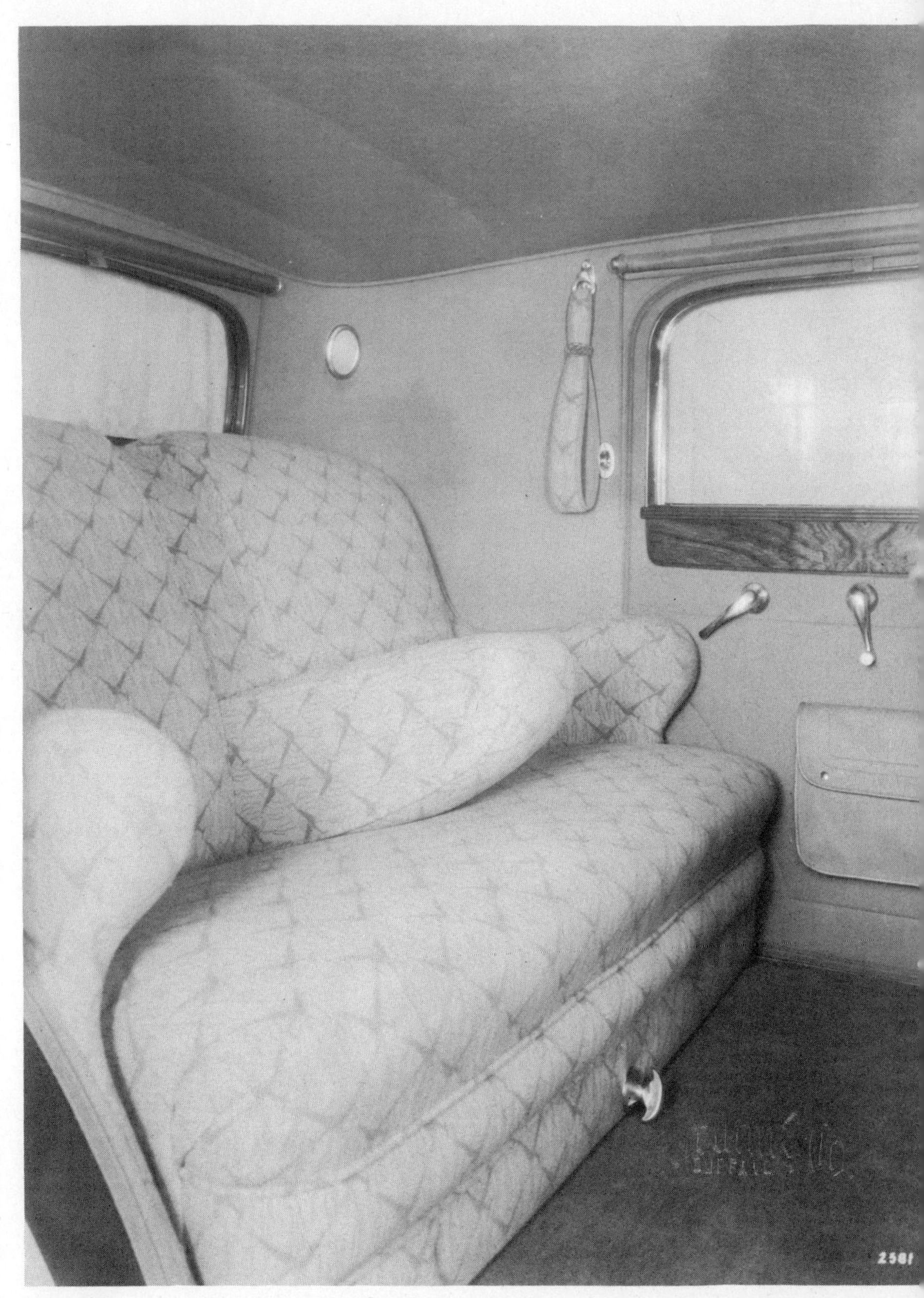

BRUNN / Lincoln / WEM

BRUNN / Lincolns / WEM

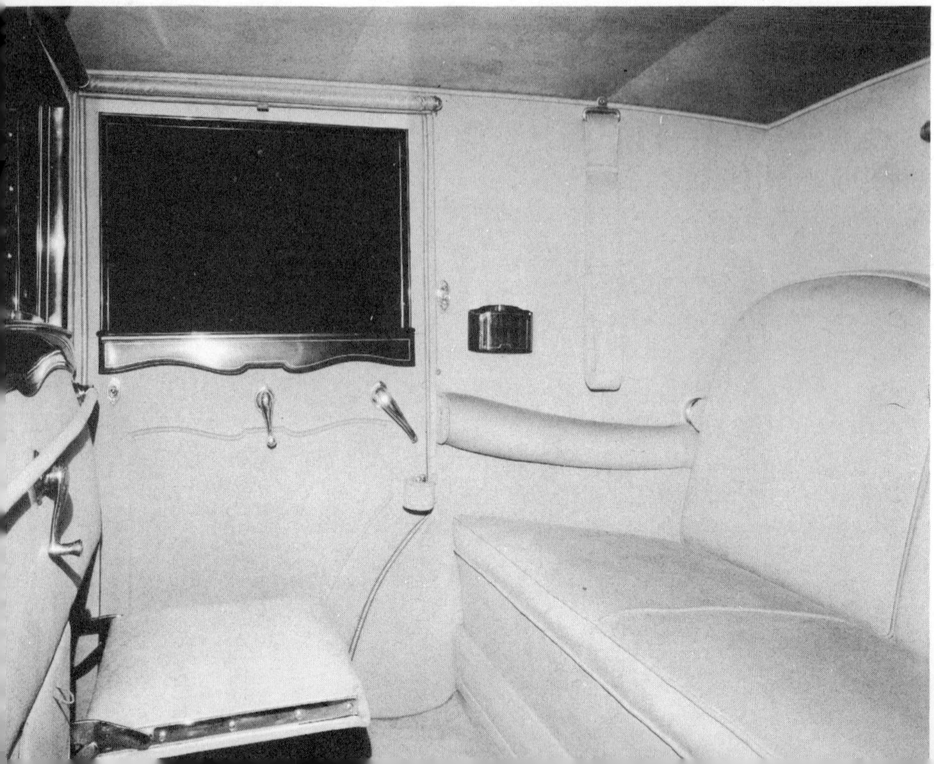

CHAPTER IX

Fitting and Making Head Lining

Owing to the fact that different weights of cloth have a different amount of stretch, the measuring of the spacing of the ribs is not practical.

The simple method is, after the cloth is cut of sufficient size, the ribs to which the listing is to be attached are selected. The cloth folded to the center is tacked temporarily at the front and the back and the ribs as selected, and marked at the selected ribs where the listing is to be placed. The folded cloth is laid on the bench and the lines squared across from the center. Lines are drawn, to which the listing is to be attached, and the listing is sewed either by machine or by hand, by "shot stitching." This method of fitting is simple and takes out just the amount of stretch required.

Where three ribs are used for the listing we must tack to the front or back of two ribs and to the opposite of the third selected rib, the center rib being tacked to first, and the first and back ribs last.

Finishing Around Front, Back and Sides

The finishing around the front, back and sides should be carefully executed, as the sewing at the listing must be kept straight. The main part of the stretching is done at the front and back, the sides being closed in naturally, no stretching being done, for the stretching would cause the head lining to "cup."

Care should also be taken where striped goods are used that they are stretched evenly, otherwise irregularity of the stripes will be caused.

Upper Quarters of a Limousine

The "upper quarters" of a limousine also comprises the upper back. A pattern is made one-half the size, of the distance from door to door, marking around where the head lining is finished at the back and quarters, around the quarter light and rear light. The material is never wide enough to make this section in one piece, so we do our piecing at the center of the rear light. The neatest method of joining is by sewing a flat seam, pressing out the seam and sewing on either side from the face.

The open space between strainers should be closed in with buckram, cardboard or canvas, over which is placed solidly a layer or two of cotton wadding. In hanging the cloth we tack temporarily, working from the center, tacking smoothly at the finish.

The stretching should be done the "up and down way" of the goods, allowing the closing in around the quarter lights and rear light to fall in naturally. Any stretching done across the goods at these points will cause the corners to lose the shape of the body.

The pillar trimming should always be padded, but the padding should be cut sufficiently far in to allow for the cord and welt finish or other finish that may be used.

Making Patterns, Cutting Cloth and Materials

In small shops there is seldom considered any system whatever, which often causes much inconvenience and waste of goods. A well-trained trimmer should endeavor to use a system which is as adaptable to a small shop as to a large one in relation to execution and economy in material.

The job should be measured and the amount of goods required ordered with the idea that no material shall be left over as waste. It is often the case in small shops that an insufficient amount of goods is ordered for a single job. Now if an order for an insufficient amount of goods is placed and more is required to finish the job the same goods may not be found in stock, consequently the trimmer proves his in-

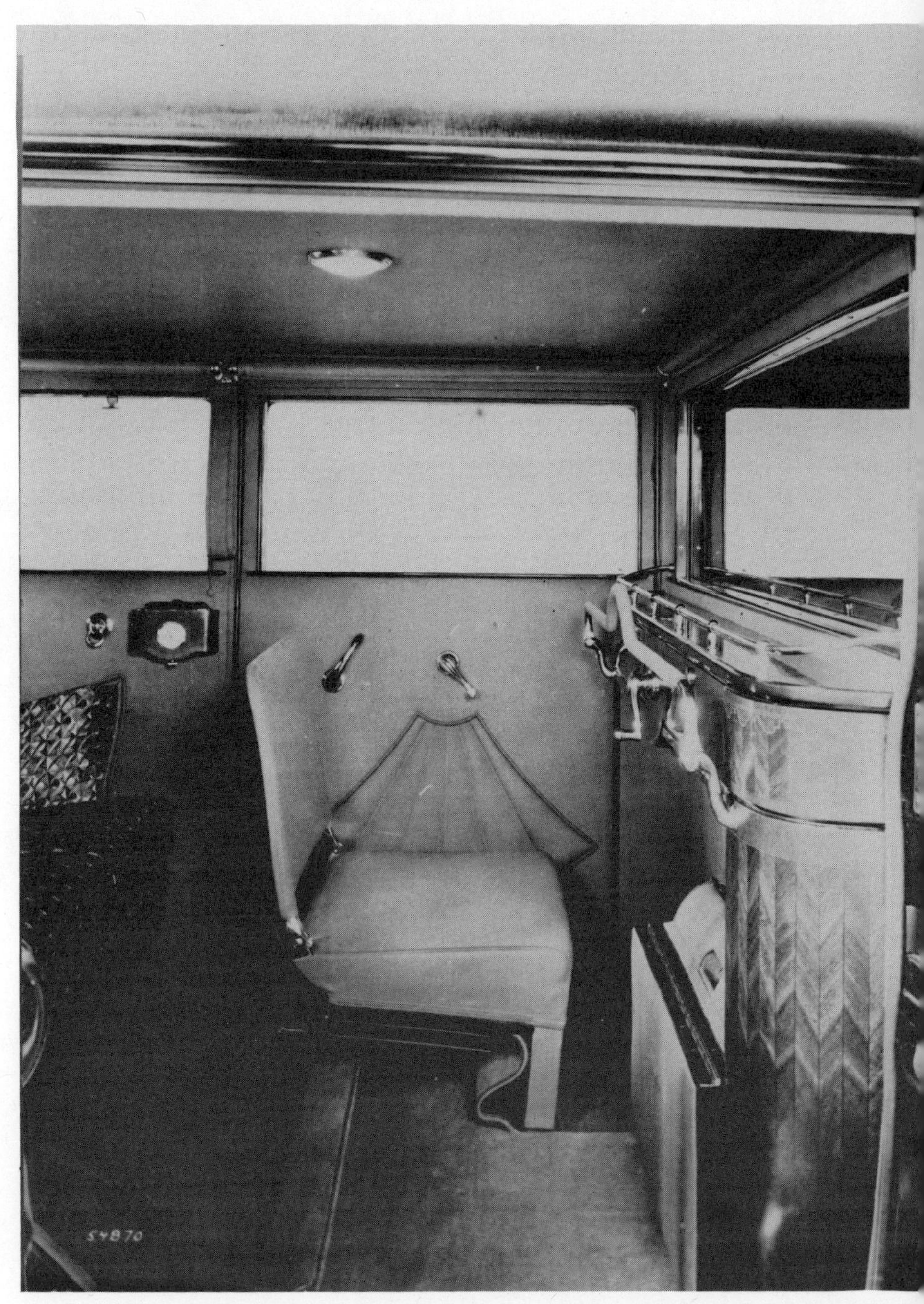

JUDKINS / Duesenberg / CWM

efficiency and puts his employer in an embarrassing position. So in buying material for a special job, be sure to get enough, but not too much.

Patterns should be made for each individual part of the trimming. Each individual part of the trimming being measured thereby allows the ordering of enough goods and no more. The cutting of material is an economical proposition and the goods for the job should be cut completely at one time.

All the patterns should be laid on the cloth and placed in such a position as to reduce waste. This not only saves time, but is the most economical method.

The trimmer should keep at all times a record of the job and the amount of material used, and this record will be useful for duplicate orders. The operating should be done at one time and not as a particular section is being made. This also saves time, not only in large shops, but in small ones as well.

Upholstered Arm Rests

Shapes and sizes of arm rests vary and are made adaptable to the job for which they are intended. Arm rests are seldom used in touring cars or cars of a like character. In limousine work there has been a tendency to reduce the size in order that the utmost room may be given to the riders.

A simple method is to use a block of wood made to the shape of drawing, which is screwed on at the proper place, over which the quarter trimming is drawn, producing a pleasing effect.

Making Door Checks

Door checks are made with the use of footman loops and harness leather, covered in the same manner as the robe rails, but are made flat instead of round, usually one and one-half inches wide. This is intended for custom work. Various methods are used for factory outputs.

JUDKINS / Lincoln / WEM
BRUNN / Lincoln / WEM

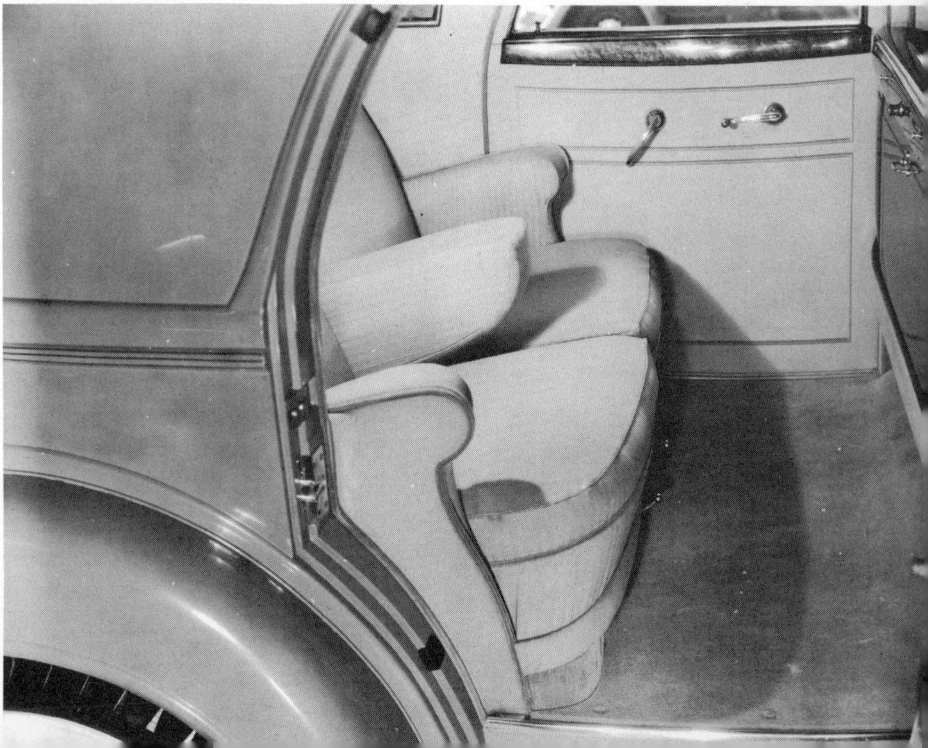

Covering Robe Rails

A robe rail is attached to the rear of the front seat partition, both on touring cars and limousines. It is intended for the carrying of blankets or coats or any other articles that may be desired for immediate use.

Robe rails are made in various ways. A simple rail permitting of rapid work and yet neat in appearance is made in this manner:

A piece of harness leather one and a half inches in width is wet and cat-stitched together; a piece of wire in the center, which is intended both to strengthen and shape the robe rail, is inserted; footman loops are used, over which the harness leather is securely fastened and the leather is then rounded to shape.

This foundation is then covered with the cloth or leather that is used for the trimming of the job and is closed in with cat-stitching. Then, again, robe rail material is furnished by upholstery makers and jobbers to match the laces.

Touring Car Doors

As much room as possible is given on touring car doors for pocket space. Very often the entire body of the door constitutes the pocket. The door is lined with canvas or other suitable material by pasting and turning the goods over the strainers.

The outer covering is then tacked to the frame of the door and the outer door trimming is made in this manner: Double-ply buckram is used as a foundation, the size of the opening of the pocket as provided for.

The foundation is fitted to the door, marked around the outer edges, cut three-quarters of an inch smaller all around, thus avoiding any obstruction to the lace or molding finish.

The outer covering of cloth or leather is pasted smoothly around the pocket opening, turned for a hem one-quarter of one inch from the edge and is ready to be tacked in place. Two layers of cotton wadding are placed over the surface of the foundation and trimmed even with the buckram. The

173

ROLLSTON / *Duesenbergs* / CWM

outer covering is then tacked smoothly in position. The flap is made on buckram, padded; outer covering hemmed and tacked in position. The door is then ready for the welt or molding finish.

If molding is used for a finish, a pattern is made the exact size of the door where the finish is required, and the molding is made from this pattern. The molding may be of nickel or brass finish, enameled black, or may be covered with the material used in trimming the job.

Lincoln / WEM

CHAPTER X

Front Seat Trimming—Plain Work

Plain trimming is much used at this time in closed car work. In fact at this writing the honors seem fairly to be divided between the French plait styles and the plain. Only where the customer especially desires it do we find examples of tufted work, but this does not mean its permanent retirement from public favor. Tufts may "come in" again. Who knows?

The plain style of trimming permits of the use of a minimum amount of hair if executed in the following manner: We will take as an example the making of a plain top front cushion which has been used with much success.

We have described the making of spring patterns and the making of springs, mentioning the gauges of wire, the pitch, and other essentials; so we will endeavor to explain only the making of a plain top cushion using a facing.

A piece of duck covering the spring, except the bottom, is used. Place temporarily in position, marking around the upper spring edge and the bottom of the cushion frame.

Draw a line one and one-half inches in from the spring edge on the front and the sides; sew to this line a piece of muslin or light duck; replace in position over the frame; whip the goods fast around the spring edge; throw in a cotton roll from one to one and one-half inches in height, which is worked to the shape of a hard roll.

The foundation material is then tacked to the wood frame of the cushion at the bottom, tacking carefully along the face edges.

The covering and roll being in position, plaited in at the corners and trimmed off at the bottom, we stitch strings across the length of the cushion in three or four equal parts, the width of the cushion, under which the hair is strung smoothly. Any irregularities in the hair are then filled in and a muslin cover is stretched over the hair, upholsterers' pins being used in this operation. After the pad is made smooth we can lightly quilt, in order to flatten or shape the surface.

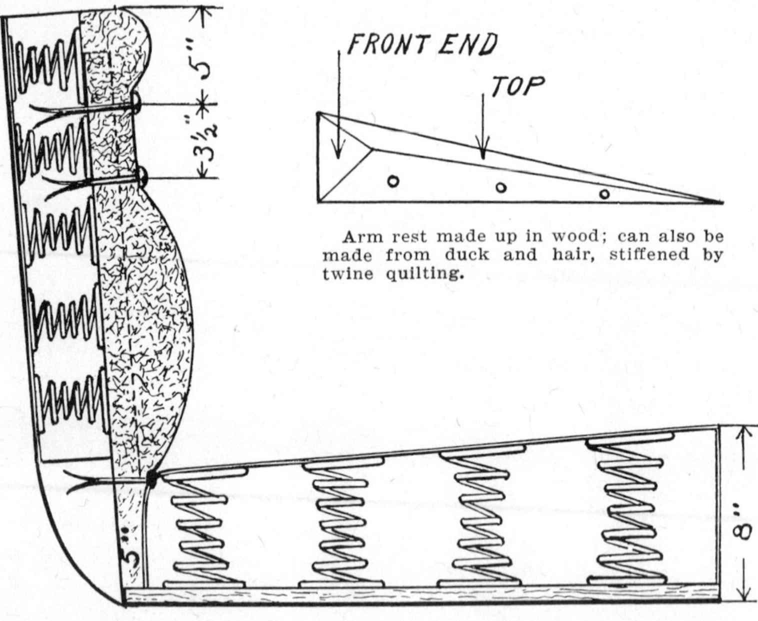

Arm rest made up in wood; can also be made from duck and hair, stiffened by twine quilting.

DIMENSION AND LOCATION DIAGRAM OF SEAT AND BACK.
May Be Used for Either Diamond Tufting or Negligee Work.

The outer edges of the muslin covering are stitched to the foundation at the sides by the use of a half-round needle. The pad being made, the leather is fitted with the use of upholsterers' pins, marked around the spring edge or where the cord is intended to finish.

The cushion facing is made by fitting a pattern around the sides, and is marked for the cord finish, as intended, around the top spring edge and the bottom of the wood framing. A sufficient amount of goods is allowed to tack underneath as a finish. Three-eighths of one inch is allowed for the cord finish at the top. The facing is then fitted, with the cord attached to the facing.

The top proper and the cord are then score-marked, so as to permit the operating to be done as fitted. The leather is then detached and the facing operated to the top.

The amount of material which has hung over in the fitting should not be trimmed off until the top and facing is again stretched into position. The surplus goods which have been left are then sewed by the use of a half-round needle to the duck foundation around the sides, underneath the spring edge. This makes it certain that the top covering will permanently hold to its position.

The facing is then drawn down and tacked underneath the wood frame, and I might mention here, lest it be overlooked, that air ventilation must be provided either by the use of grommets placed at the side and rear of the facing or in the bottom covering.

A cushion made in this manner proves successful, allows the cushion spring to have its absolute freedom and the "full of its life" and permits a minimum amount of materials to be used.

Two pounds of hair would be the maximum amount required by making over the spring. Were the pad to be made on a frame, more material and more time would be required.

Making Front Back in the Plain Style

In trimming a plain back over the springs, the following method proves effective: The spring is placed in position, covered with a layer of duck, tacked to the wood framing of the seat and at the top rail, stringing across. Under the strings is placed the hair.

The hair is piled to the desired shape; an outer covering is placed over the hair, tacked to the seat frame at the bottom and at the top rail. A sufficient amount of goods is left on the ends to turn in, thus forming a pocket. The pad is then quilted through to avoid the shifting of hair.

The leather or other material is then tacked over the foundation, covered with a layer of cotton, tacked first to the seat board, drawn tightly to the top finish and turned in at the ends. This forms a well-constructed, comfortable back, with the use of a minimum amount of hair.

The finish is accomplished by the use of lace or metal molding. This style of back is built at a less cost than a back made on a frame with a pad.

The finishing off of a job has a great deal to do with the impression created. A body may be exceptionally well trimmed, but if the laces, welts, etc., are not tightly drawn, smoothly laid and evenly tacked, the entire effect is lost. It perhaps is one of the hardest operations in trimming a body, requiring the utmost patience and extreme neatness. Even a good trimmer will find it a nice test of his ability.

Lincoln / WEM

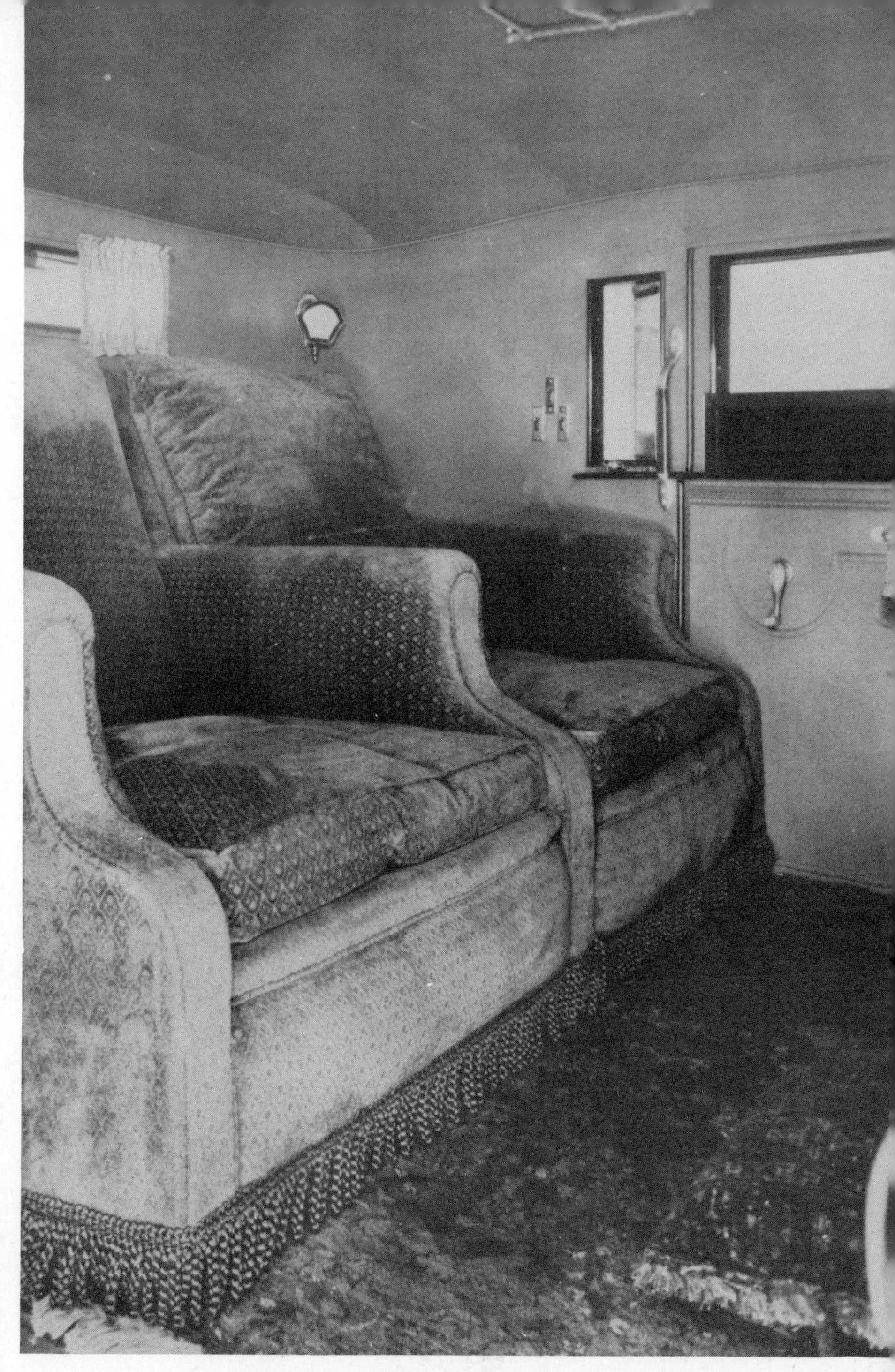

WATERHOUSE / Rolls-Royce PI / MMcC

WATERHOUSE / Rolls-Royce PI / MMcC

CHAPTER XI

Some Notes on Slip Covers

It is our purpose to treat of a job as received in a custom shop for top and slip covers, where first-class high-grade work is done. The method we propose to explain, both as to top and slip covers, is one which might be adapted to large-scale production with the use of patterns.

In making patterns for slip covers for duplication, all parts must be fitted and basted. The sections, such as the backs, quarters, cushions or other parts, which must be shaped to the upholstering, must be basted on the job while being fitted. After the basting the goods are trimmed off, 3/8-inch allowance being made for the beading. A spring punch (a No. 1 punch) is used to make guide holes for joining by the operator.

After the shaped parts are fitted completely and accurately they are taken apart and from this fitting the patterns are made for duplication.

Use of Templates on Quantity Work

Generally upholstery work is so accurately made by the use of templates on standard factory built jobs that slip lining is not only possible, but very easy. We will endeavor to explain the making of a slip lining in the most simple manner as made in a high-class custom shop and which method can be used for duplication or quantity work.

Rough patterns should be cut for all separate sections for slip lining. The cutting of patterns for the cutting of the goods saves material. All parts should be cut at one time after rough patterns are secured. Cutting all goods at the one time saves much material and labor.

Interior Fitted with Slip Covers for Summer Use

The section at the rear of the back, say, for instance, the rear back, where the fasteners are placed for the back curtain and side curtains, which constitutes the center of the rear back and side quarters, should be fitted first. Leather is used as the top section over the quarters. The outside parts should be fitted and sewed together at the corners.

That part of the top which constitutes the center part should be fitted and sewed together at the corners. These two sections are basted together and then the bottom part of the quarters and back is fitted and sewed together at the center part of the radius. This is then tacked in position and stretched tightly and basted to the two previous sections which have already been placed and basted into position.

Mark around the bottom, allowing an inch or so for tacking to the wood seat framing, where the parts are basted together. Trim off about five-sixteenths inch from the basting. A spring punch is used (a No. 1 punch) punching through in spaces close to the outer edge, as trimmed. This gives a guide line for the operator and eliminates the use of chalk. Chalk is often undesirable as an operator's guide from the fact that chalk marks are hard to remove.

Most all slip linings today are welted, so in order to welt the work the stitches must be removed and the goods turned the opposite way from that on which it was basted.

The outer edge of the rear back section is bound with manufacturer's binding, that is to say, a binding prepared by manufacturers with one edge cemented and turned. This permits of a neat, flat binding with the outside stitching showing, and is rapidly done by an expert operator, and no basting or turning is required. The welting is five-eighths to three-quarters inch wide and is also furnished by manufacturers of welting in 100-yard rolls.

The front seat is fitted and finished in the same manner. The fasteners used are of various makes, all of which are good if they are easy to attach and hold the lining close to the job. First-class custom slip linings are usually attached by the means of such fasteners, and tacks are seldom used.

Doors and other flat parts are fitted to cover the upholstery, reinforced around the edges to give strength to the fasteners and finished with the flat binding.

It is well when beginning to make a job of slip lining work, especially where leather is the upholstery to be covered, that the lines intended for the welting should be marked off on the job, with chalk, thus laying out your lines for basting in keeping with the shape of the job.

In fitting for the cushions, mark off with chalk on the cushion top where the beading is intended to be placed. Take the goods cut for the top and pin in place with the use of upholsterers' clamps. The lines intended for the beading should be placed far enough in from the outer edges so that all the beading may show.

A slip lining for a cushion looks much neater with the welting all around the top rather than attempting the faceless front, and holds its shape much better.

Where the cushion is nearly square the side facings are not required to be fitted, but where the pitch is two inches or more the facing must be fitted to get a smooth job. Otherwise with a square cushion, the size of the top piece being gotten out, a facing could be sewed around with the beading without fitting. But where the facing is fitted it is shaped to the cushion, basted to the top and sewed together.

The bottom of the cushion is marked off, folded over on the bottom at the front, mitered at the back corners underneath and hemmed as a bottom finish. Straps of the same material are made in three-fold, three-quarter inch in width, three straps across cushion. Fasten with skate buckles.

For children's seats, the backs are usually fitted and made the same as a flat bag and closed with a flat binding, glove fasteners closing in the bottom. The seat proper is usually mitered at the corners, turned over at the bottom and the bottom closed with a flat, square piece with glove fasteners.

The goods required for slip-covering a seven-passenger job averages fifteen yards of fifty-inch material. Time required, first-class work, one man completing the job, forty-five hours.

CHAPTER XII

Trimming Cape Top for Touring Car

Various methods are pursued in top building which are governed by shop conditions and output. Custom work tops are built on the job, but top work for duplication is ofttimes built with the use of a "buck"; that is to say, a framework is built to represent the body irons and shape of back of job, also representing the windshield.

But the use of a "buck" sometimes proves to be a failure unless they are made heavy and absolutely rigid. The better method, where large output is concerned, is to use a model body with windshield attached and fasteners placed in the job, and the entire top can be completed.

The boots are made from patterns and do not require a fitting for each individual job. After the bodies are trimmed the fasteners can be placed to fit the rear and side curtains by the use of templates.

There are various shapes of tops, the bows having different positions, different styles of back curtains, different shapes of quarters, but all are intended to harmonize with the job for which they are built.

A wonderful selection of top materials is obtainable, each material having its particular virtue. There are various patented methods for curtain arrangements and curtains to swing open with the doors by the means of removable rods are made. The most satisfactory curtains in use today are the last mentioned, and when made by an up-to-date trimmer please the most critical.

Setting the Bows on a Touring Car Top

In building a touring car top on custom work this procedure is followed, but the same method can be used in obtaining measurements, patterns and amount of goods required. The top is first set, giving the proper "over hang" at the rear and the pitch of the bows, which on the ordinary touring top is five inches on the front and two and one-half to three inches on the rear.

Bows.—A piece of non-stretchable webbing is tacked on the front, second, third and rear bows to hold the top in shape. The pads are then stretched in position.

We might make reference to a little "stunt" that helps to keep the wrinkles and draws out of the pad. The back part of the pad is made wider than the front and a seam is stitched the length of the pad in the center. This helps wonderfully in making a smooth pad.

The pads being tacked in position, four lengths of non-stretchable webbing is placed over the pad and about four or five layers of cotton wadding tapered off at the edges and cut from over the bows and tapered, over which the pad covering material is stretched. This is joined together by stitching.

In laying on the cotton padding each layer of cotton should be touched with paste. The strainers across the bows, if used, are stretched into position. The cutting of the materials should be done at the same time. That is, marking out on the goods of the different sections, and then cutting them.

The quarters are then fitted and should be stretched tightly and smoothly; the quarter line is marked out and the deck stretched over the quarters, turned under at the edges at the seam lines, and marked with chalk and checked for operating. Care should be taken that both the quarters and the deck are stretched in position with equal strain.

After the fitting the goods are removed and a reinforcement sewed along the bottom of the quarters, which is intended for the fasteners of the curtains, if they are required.

A good finish for the quarters is of leather to match the goods, made as a flat binding. The back curtain is fitted and marked for the fasteners and curtain lights.

A sufficient amount of goods should be left below the edge of the body to close tightly when placed in position.

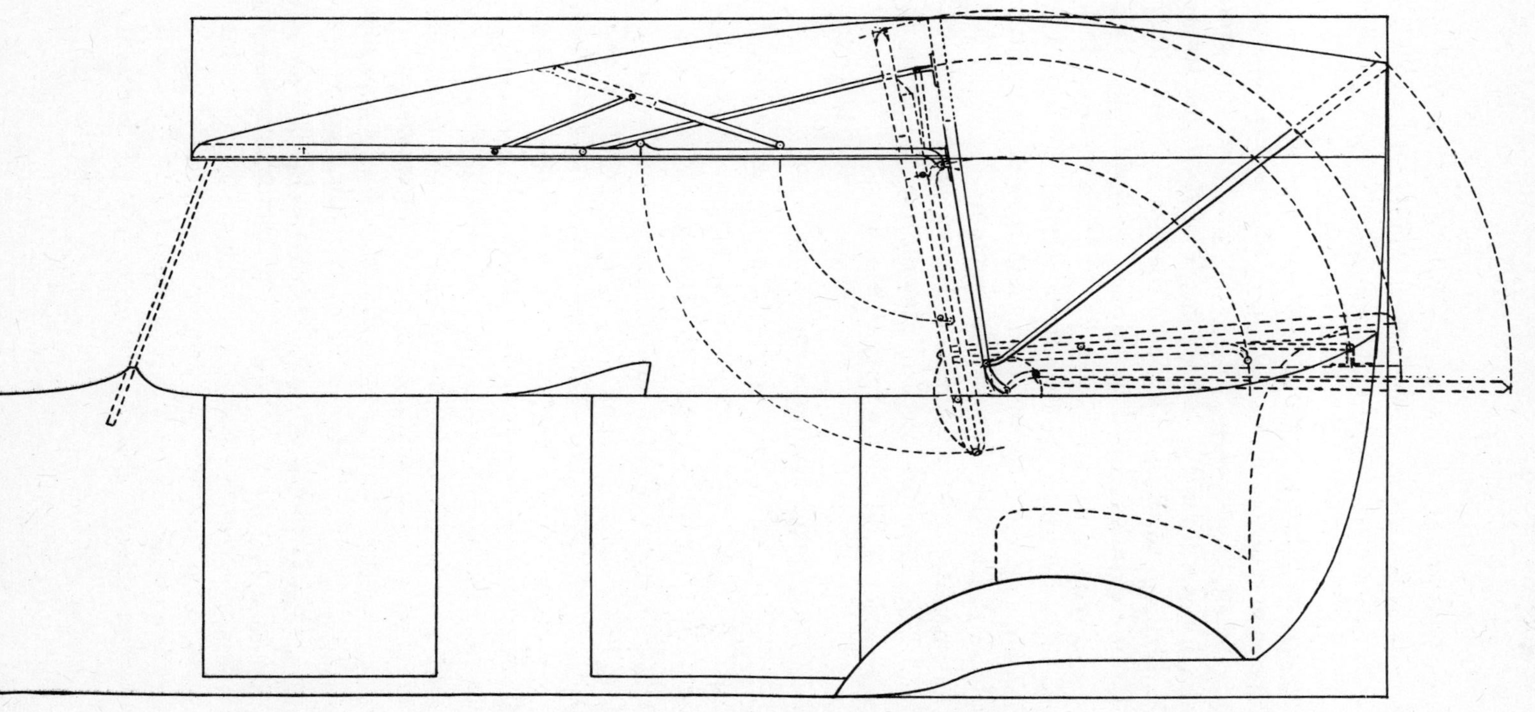

Diagram Illustrating the Proper Setting of a "One-Man" Top

Backstay strips are most reliable if made of harness leather to match the material, which are attached by means of footman loops on the bow and body, with a buckle provided to take up the play.

The top and back curtains, having been duly operated, are drawn and tacked into position. The quarters and back curtain being bound with leather, the finish for the front and back bows should be a cord made of the same leather as the binding, to which is added a metal-covered molding.

The side curtains should be finished with a leather binding. All side curtains should be reinforced around the edges. The windbrake beyond the windshield should be made of metal, covered with the same material and fitting closely to the windshield when in position.

The amount of goods required is thirteen yards of 60-inch goods. Time required for custom work, one man doing the work completely, is about forty-five hours.

Making Patterns for Duplication

In making patterns for duplication, as each section is completed and found to be correct, it should be transferred to a pattern, that is to say, strainer lengths can be obtained, pad sizes, curtains cut and bound, quarters cut and bound, back curtains cut and bound, lights placed in the same, all made up, laid away and ready for each top as soon as the bows are set up and the pads are built. The quarters and deck are bound and ready to be fitted and the deck seams joined together by the operators and are ready as soon as the back curtains are placed in position.

This method is used when tops are being built over sample bodies or "bucks." When bows are required to be covered with leather they are done in advance and ready for the particular job as it comes along. So by using this method top builders can be kept continually assembling without interruption.

CHAPTER XIII

An Economical Spring Cushion

Motor car upholstery can be very economically done through the use of properly made and arranged spring construction and manufactured cotton batts.

The spring construction required is of the lace web type, made to the shape of the back required and the shape of the cushion required, woven across with wire netting where the covering of upholstery comes in contact with the springs.

Spirals of course are used and are held in position by wire supports. The spring is covered over with a light duck or burlap covering, over which is stretched the French plait style of work filled with cotton batts. If the spring construction is properly manufactured and properly shaped a satisfactory degree of comfort and durability is obtained.

In making a cushion of this type, the back would be made along the same lines. We would suggest the following method: The springs should be made the height and size required. The top covering of the spring should be of closely woven net work. The French plait style of work is made up in the usual manner.

A good, heavy thickness of cotton batt is pushed in the plait and is fitted over the spring and marked off at the back, the sides and the bottom of the frame. The spring is attached to a wood frame with staples. The material at the bottom of the front is allowed to turn-under and is tacked to the wood frame. At the sides and back it is marked around the spring edge, to which the facing with cord attached is fitted and sewed to the top by machine.

The spring should be covered with a good, heavy layer of cotton, over which the top is stretched and attached to the wood framing at the bottom and finished off with either a covering of canvas or manufactured lace.

Ventilation must not be overlooked at the bottom or the rear and side facings. This will complete an acceptable cushion for the cheaper grades of work without the use of hair.

Notes on Repair Work

Where an apprentice is connected with a custom shop or jobbing shop a wonderful opportunity for his development is afforded in repair work, where trimming must be removed and replaced, thus affording him an opportunity to acquaint himself with the materials used and being, so to speak, a preliminary education.

The removing of upholstery must be done with judgment and care. Tacks should be lifted and entirely removed from the cloth. The upholstery should never be pulled until the tacks have been lifted, and if no marks are visible for the position of the upholstery, guide lines should be placed thereon to insure the replacing of the upholstery in exactly the same position from which it is removed.

Tacks should never be left in the upholstery as removed, for the reason that they are very apt to pierce the cloth or scratch the leather, and if by accident they should be carelessly handled the goods may be ripped or some trimmer is likely to have a cut finger.

The handling of repair work by an apprentice acquaints him with the various parts and styles and different methods of doing the work, and gives him much food for thought.

TRIMMING OPERATIONS CLASSIFIED

Automobile trimming may be divided into the following branches or operations:

CUTTING ROOM

Creating the design.

Making the patterns.

Laying out the foundation patterns.

Laying out the fullness patterns.

Cutting of the materials.

Getting out rough stuff as foundations for doors, quarter pads or other parts that require pasting and drying.

OPERATING ROOM

All sewing that is to be done.

BENCH WORK

Cushion making.

Back making.

Quarter making.

Auxiliary seat trimming.

Hassock making.

Curtain making.

Carpet making.

Lace making.

Robe rail and door check making.

Welt making.

BODY TRIMMING

Trimming above the belt line.

Back and quarter hanging.

Door trimming.

Cowl trimming.

Finishing, such as lacing off, hanging curtains, robe rails, door checks, pull-to handles and other detachable or removable parts.

Separately trained workmen can be used to work the above system successfully, permitting the specializing of operators for each particular branch of trimming.

Many of the above operations may also be sub-divided where the production is sufficiently large to warrant a subdivision. By this method, together with the proper supervision and distribution of materials and work, costs can be maintained at a minimum.

WEYMANN / Duesenberg / CWM

CHAPTER XIV

Complete Trimming of a Typical Enclosed Car

In the pages that have preceded, we have confined our instructions to the broad, general principles of motor car upholstery. In other words, we have outlined general methods with wide application to the different types of cars.

Now, as an illustration of the complete trim of a car from start to finish, we will take up a particular type of body and discuss it in its entirety. We have selected for this purpose one of the most popular styles of closed bodies, the reason for this choice being that in a closed car we perform virtually all the operations necessary in an open car (with the exception of the folding top) and besides have the advantage of reviewing the principles involved in trimming the upper parts and the head lining of the closed car, which are not to be found in cars of the touring and roadster types. We will proceed to describe the upholstering of a sedan, in the French plait style.

A sedan, as defined in the dictionary, is a covered, portable chair for carrying a single person, but as used today in the automobile industry it is the name of an automobile body with a permanent roof and carrying numerous persons. The characteristic features of the automobile sedan are:

First—A car for all seasons.

Second—A family car.

Third—Adaptability for owner's personal driving.

Fourth—Sociability features.

Fifth—Roomy passenger accommodation without crowding.

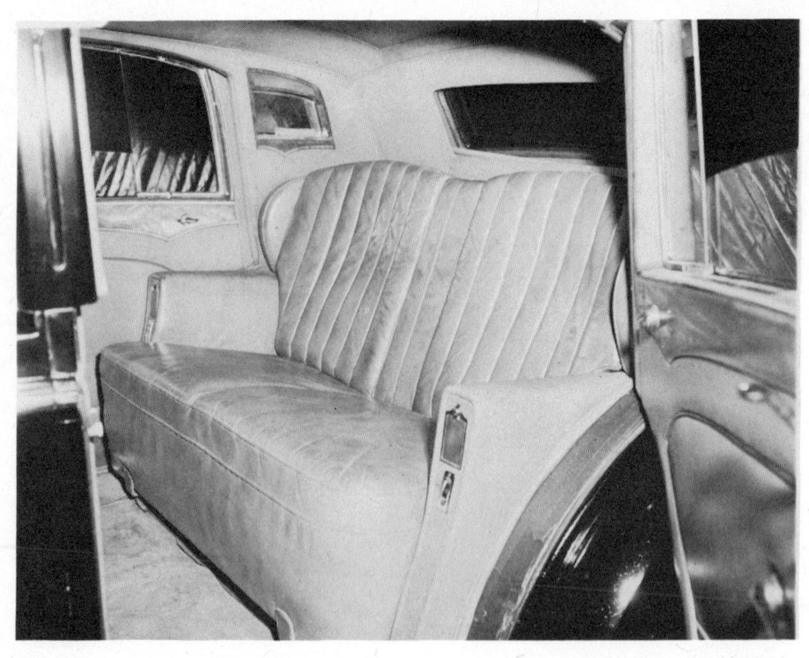

MULLINER / Rolls-Royce / WBD

Advantages of the Sedan Body

We find in the sedan body many valuable and important features which put it in a class by itself. As an all-season car it is indeed more valuable than the open or so-called touring body. It affords considerably more protection in cold and stormy weather than the touring body, yet in clear, warm weather permits of all the ventilation necessary. Some types are fully as open as any touring car, with the exception that the roof is permanent, and it is even now an open question as to whether or not the permanent roof is not an advantage.

The Sedan a "Family" Car

As a family car the sedan is indeed winning great success. For mother and children feel more certain when touring, that should a storm arise the car can be closed up tightly and they are as safe and dry as they would be at home.

The sedan also affords all the conveniences of any other enclosed body with the additional features of being adapted for the owner's personal driving. The owner may drive a sedan, yet be "one of the party"; he may enjoy conversation with his family or guests without being isolated and made to appear in the rôle of chauffeur on the job.

For touring, theatre parties or visiting, the sedan, as a family car for the owner who likes to drive, is the logical body. With it he gets all the features of the touring car and limousine without the disadvantage of being made to feel like a chauffeur. Then again, due to the construction of a sedan and the seating arrangements, the owner of the car may take with him five or six guests, and they are all together, and may enjoy the social advantages incident to the occasion. None are isolated and none are separated by a partition from any of the others.

The sedan body, for the owner who likes to drive, becomes not unlike a living room on wheels. It may be adopted for all uses—to take the family on a tour; an evening or Sunday drive; for the theatre party or a trip down town. He may take his friends with him and enjoy the benefit of their company and they his. The car may be used in business. Its construction permits of more room than any other type of body, and the backs and cushions may be made as deep and as comfortable as the big arm chair in front of the fireplace at home.

Owning and driving a sedan, with the benefit of congenial company, together with a drive through the country, broadens a man's mind, educates him and really makes life one round of pleasure, in addition to keeping the family healthy by getting them out in the air and permitting them to enjoy the beauties of nature.

Can you imagine anything more satisfying, giving more pleasure than a drive through the country when the leaves are turning and all the world seems like a riot of color, the air sharp and snappy—yet you and yours are warm and comfortable in a big, roomy, well-upholstered sedan?

We shall ask you to imagine taking a trip in a seven-passenger roomy sedan (mounted on any good chassis) painted battleship gray—and for a sedan that is a mighty good color—upholstered partly in cloth and partly in gray Spanish leather or a good leather substitute.

The cloth is of harmonious color to match or harmonize with the paint and leather. The cushions are deep, well made and comfortable. The backs well shaped, and giving absolute ease and rest.

The style of upholstering used is the genuine French plait. The front seats are trimmed in leather or leather substitute. The roof and all above the belt line is trimmed in the same material, and the rear seat, quarters and doors, up to the belt line, are trimmed in cloth.

The floor is covered with a good grade of gray carpet, in the form of a rug, the reverse side being lined with rubber for stormy weather. The body is thoroughly equipped with all the up-to-date mountings and appurtenances.

PARK WARD / Rolls-Royce / WBD

An Opportunity for the Trimmer's Skill

To really make the sedan the enjoyable body it should be, the trimmer has a wonderful opportunity for displaying his skill. Since this description is primarily for the benefit of the trimmer, we shall now endeavor to treat in detail the trimming of such a body.

The first consideration in the trimming of a sedan is to lay out the plans in order that all necessary equipment be at hand when the job is placed at the trimmer's bench. By this we mean that the material necessary must be ordered in advance and be in stock when the job is ready to trim—springs, cloth, carpet and all necessary equipment—so there shall be no unnecessary delay in completing the job.

Making the Spring Patterns for Cushion

The spring patterns should be made before the job is ready to trim, in fact, should be done as soon as the job is far enough along in its construction to permit their being correctly made. In making the spring patterns a cheap grade of thin canvas may be used. The use of canvas is recommended rather than paper because of the nature of canvas; it is more adaptable to the "folding in" and marking and can be more readily preserved and filed for future use.

In marking the pattern, allowances should be made at the quarters and at the back, taking into consideration the absolute freedom of the spring. By this is meant that no resistance shall be offered the spring, due to its contact or binding at the quarters or at the back, thus permitting all the resiliency possible.

That the springs shall be just right is a very important matter. In order that all the room possible may be given (considering that the back should have ample depth) the measurements as laid down by experience should be 5/8 of one inch on each side and 1 1/2 inches at the rear, thus giving ample freedom for the back.

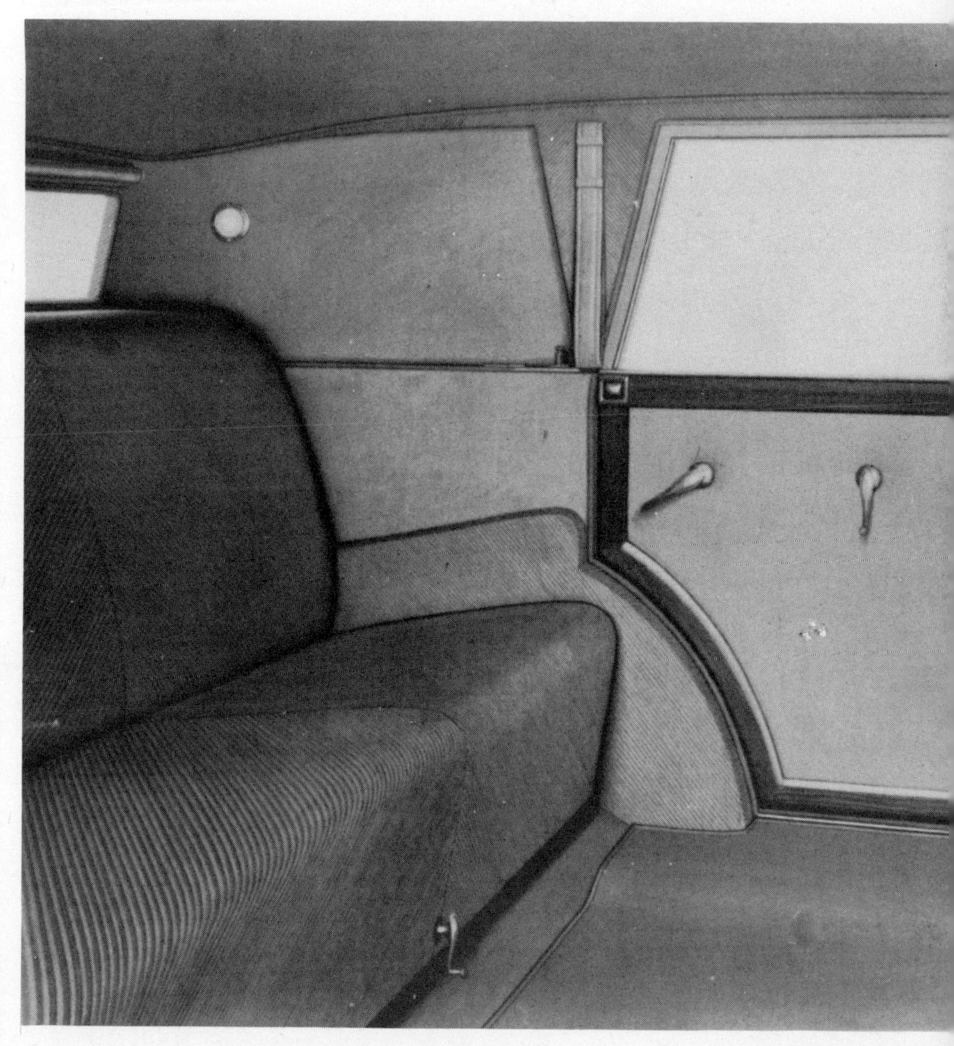

Duesenberg / WCK

We consider that the proper pitch under the present demand should be 3 inches, or the front of the spring should be 8 inches, while the rear of the spring should be 5 inches. In these measurements we take into consideration not only the pitch of the spring but also the height, so as to offer sufficient resistance to take the bumps and jars of high-speed traveling. After the patterns are made for duplication, patterns should be preserved. We do not mean preservation of the pattern for the cushion only, but of all other patterns, because in large shops the trimmer is always called upon for measurements in order that duplication can be made.

The Back Springs

In this particular type of body we are considering comfort as well as roadability and durability. As much attention, if not more, should be given to the proper construction of the back. In order to have absolute freedom, clearance must be provided for at the sides in making the pattern for the back spring, which we are now considering to be of the manufactured type. It is much better to have more room on the side for spring action than not enough. One inch should be absolutely free of the quarters, thus giving ample space for the building in of the back when placed in the job.

Building Up the Backs

The old methods of building in the backs are now not in vogue, as a spring construction is placed in the job and the back pad is built up in the job instead of being made up on the bench as formerly.

The method now used in building the back is that of placing the spring construction in the desired position, then tacking a first covering of 10-ounce duck, soft buckram or other suitable material. The spring being covered, it is pressed into the desired position. Care should be taken that the forward or outer framework of the spring construction is placed in such a position that the spring will not sag downward, or in other words, the spring when placed in

ROLLSTON / Duesenberg "Twenty Grand" / CWM

position should be caused to work on its absolute centers. The spring when in this position should be whipped fast to the upper and lower frame construction. This method holds in place the spring, eliminating all shifting.

The spring now being in position, use the curved needle. Some of the "boys" term these the "half moon" needle. Twine it across in four equal spaces. Twine in the hair, placing it in such a position and in sufficient amount that no trace of the spring may be felt, then draw on outer covering of the same duck or buckram. Build the back to the desired shape.

Covering the Backs

The back is then ready for the placing of the outer covering. In building a back of this description it is necessary that the sides should be given due consideration so that no hair may work out. This is accomplished by throwing the surplus material at the sides, which the trimmer terms a "pocket." When the outer covering is placed, all that is necessary is that sufficient goods be allowed to throw in between the back and quarters.

The style of the front backs in this particular type of car is that of the rounded or Pullman seats. In the building of these backs, owing to the "round" in the back and the small amount of space permitted for spring arrangement, the writer prefers the use of the old method of sewing in the springs on buckram or cardboard, being bridled or tied in by the use of spring twine to the desired shape. While the writer prefers to take into consideration the driver and his companion, it is not possible, due to the construction of the job, to give as much spring construction as is deemed necessary.

The building in of the front backs after the springs are placed in position is accomplished by the same methods as used in the rear back. While the cushion springs for the front, owing to the fact that there is less swell in the backs, require less play at the rear, in this case one inch freedom is ample.

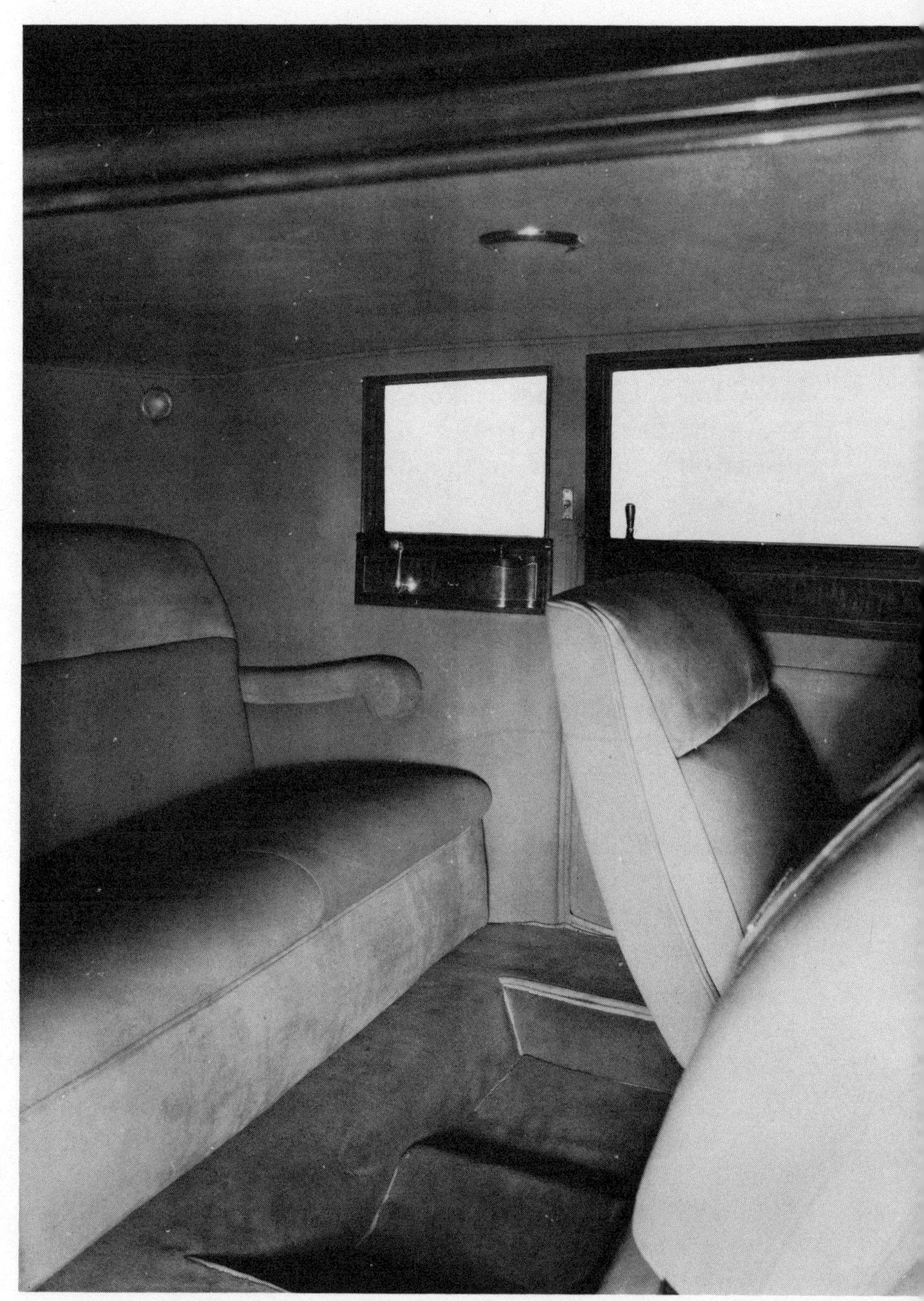

ROLLSTON / Duesenberg / WCK

Head Lining, Quarters and Above Belt Line

Methods of trimming are modified by experience. Quantity of production materially affects systems and methods in the different classes of trim shops. Where large outputs are handled and where different grades of mechanics follow one another in the completion of the job, the writer prefers to use the method of "above the belt line first."

First place the upper rear quarters and cover all the upright pillars. The fact that the head lining is hung after the trimming is placed in position above the belt line, gives more freedom to the workmen. As this job is trimmed above the belt line in leather or leather substitute, the process of fitting the head lining most advisable is that of selecting the ribs on which to tack the listing, placing the leather or other material in such a position that the ribs may be marked. This method is more absolute than that of measuring because the nature of some leather as well as leather cloth is to have more stretch than others.

The manner of tacking and finishing the head lining is that which is well known to all proficient trimmers and is best learned by watching a good trimmer actually do the work. The listing should be allowed sufficient drop at the ribs so that no impression appears. The method used in attaching the leather or leather substitute head lining to the listing is by machine stitching from the face side. The finishing around the sides, front and back, should be given slightly more than the depth of the ribs.

Trimming the Quarters

All above the belt line now being trimmed, then follows the placing of the quarters. We are trimming this job in the well-known French plait style. It is usually considered that the French plait style is the next thing to plain work, and some relief should be given to plainness.

We are also considering as much room for the passenger as is possible in the construction of the body, yet some little relief should be given, and provision should be made for

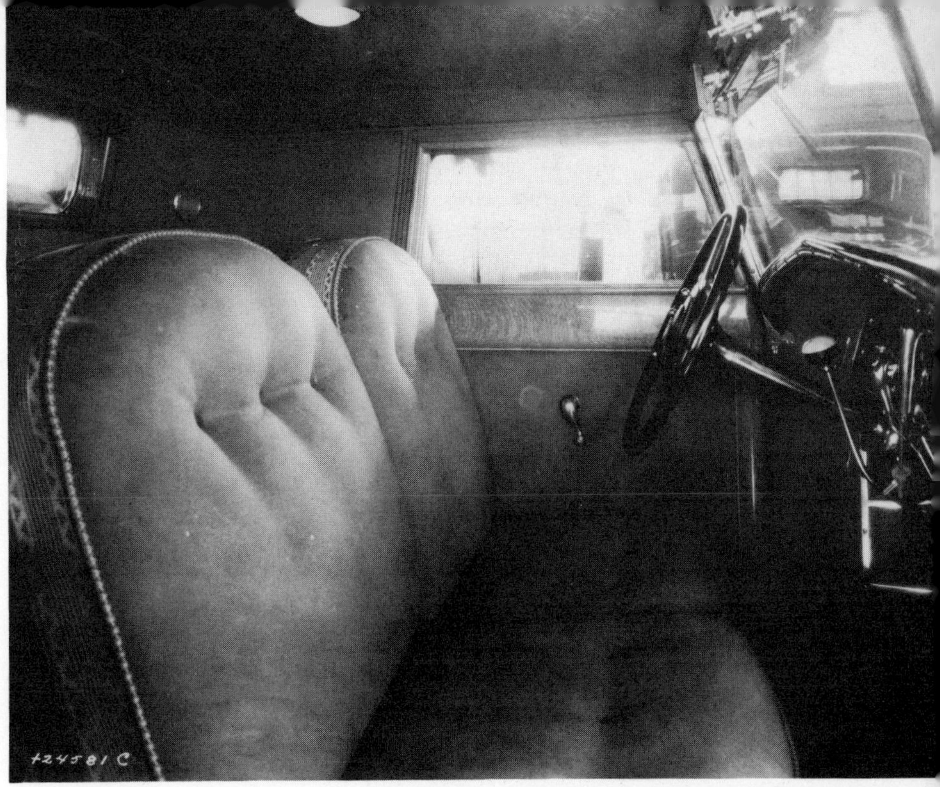

WALKER-LE GRANDE / Duesenberg / CWM
ROLLSTON / Duesenberg / CWM

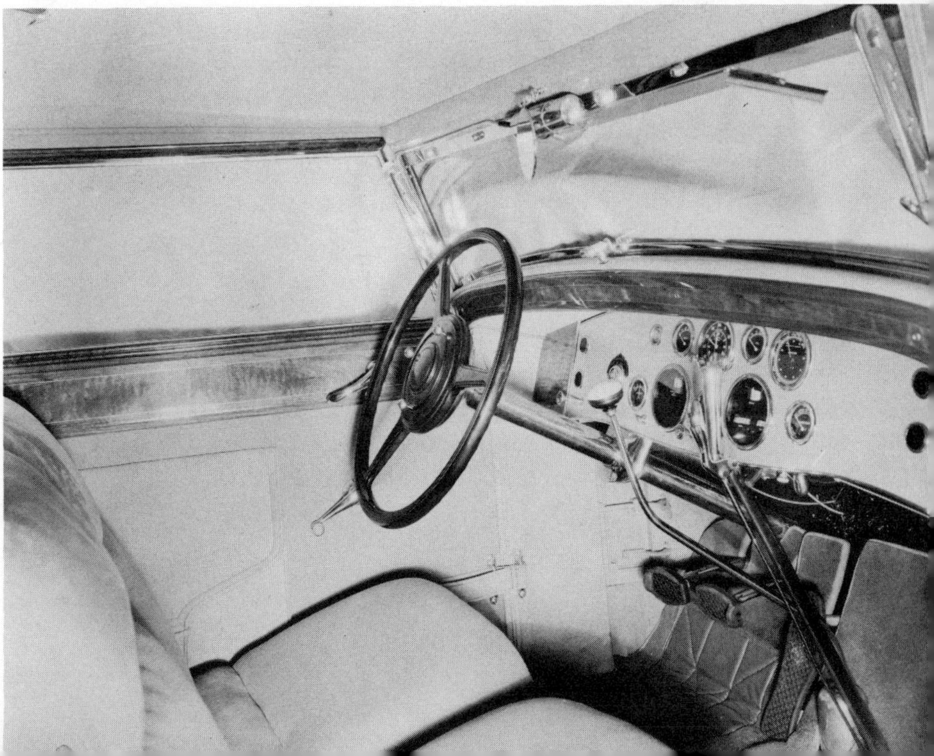

an arm rest. But the object of the arm rest at the present time is only to relieve the appearance of plainness, or in other words, the arm rest should be made as small as possible, yet should be made in such a way that there is a semblance of a rest. The same effect is accomplished by the use of a wood block, triangular in shape, about 2½ inches at the top and 2½ inches in height at the front, tapering back about twelve inches to a feather edge. A listing is sewed on the quarters, over which the arm rest is placed in position, thus holding the quarters in closely to the sides. The goods are thrown over the top in position, and the finish obtained is both pleasing to the eye and permits the trimmer to display neatness and skill.

In the lining up of the back and quarters the curve desired is that of a graceful, easy, comfortable chair, which result is obtained by taking the height of the back at the center of the rear and curving in at the side at the position of the arm rest.

We consider in the trimming of all work the length of service it is to endure and make provision accordingly, namely: the protection of the trimming when the car is repainted, hence we place at all outer edges, where coming in contact with the paint, a leather beading or cord in keeping with the color of the upholstering, against which is placed the flat welt of the same material in which the car is trimmed. The reason we are making flat welts of the same material as the cloth or leather used, is because worsted laces and molding are now seldom used.

Carpet Covers the Entire Floor

The carpet of the sedan, owing to the construction, permits of an entire covering of the floor, giving a "home-like" appearance. Certain manufacturers specialize on carpets made especially for automobiles, offering a wide range of patterns and colors, and in the exact widths to fit any car.

Drafts or patterns for the laying out of the work can be

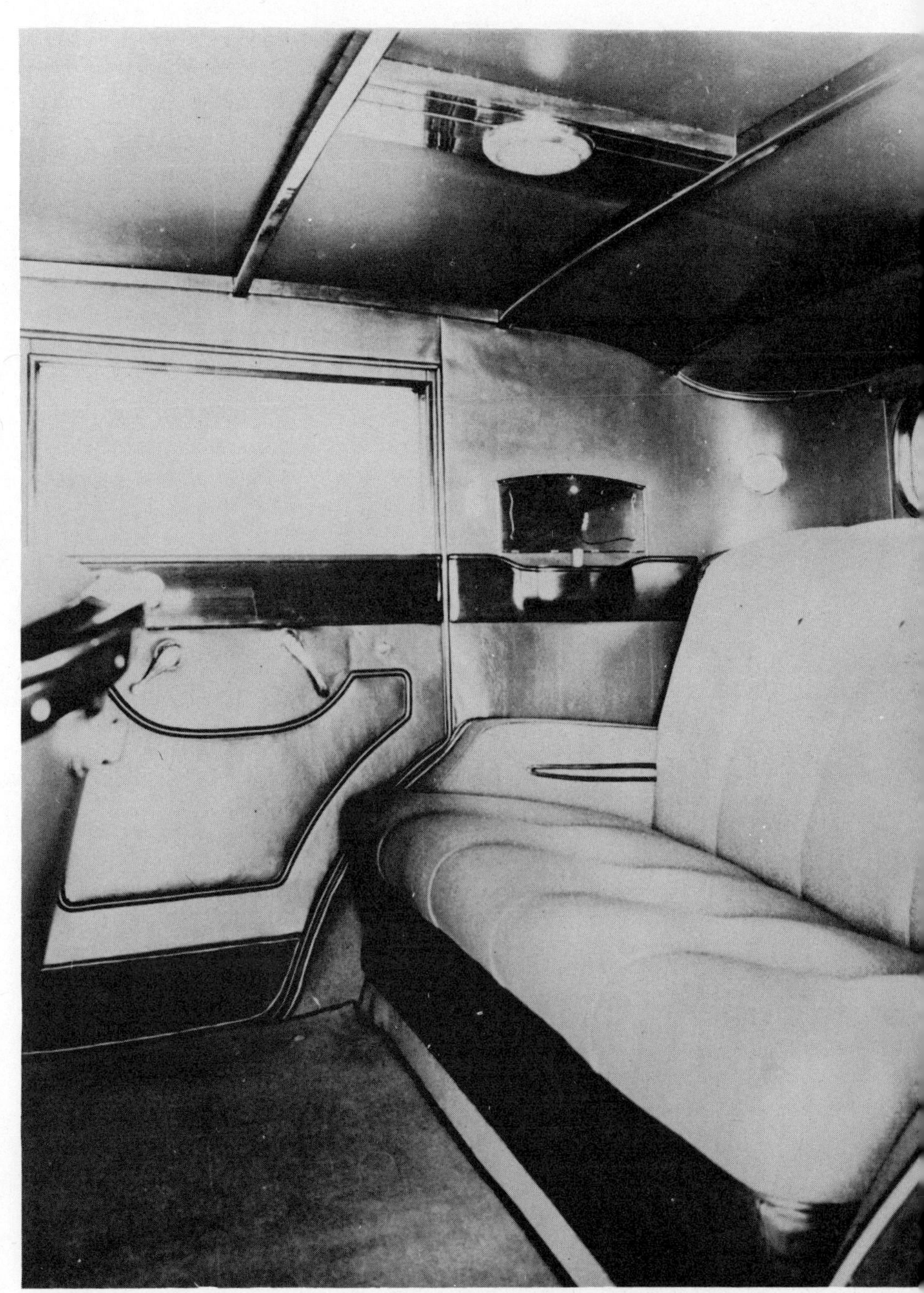

DERHAM / Duesenberg "Arlington" / CWM

referred to in previous chapters in this book, but we might mention that in the French plait style, the plait should be as near as possible to 3½ inches in width. The fullness required is ⅝ of an inch, thus permitting the filling up of the plait with layers of cotton batting which will completely fill this amount of fullness. This comment refers to the genuine French plait. The covering of cushion keepers and other small details is left entirely to the judgment of the trimmer, considering, of course, the construction of the body he may be trimming. The construction of the typical sedan is such that two doors only are usually to be trimmed. The back cushion and quarters, as well as the front backs and cushions, are French plait; the doors should be trimmed plain with the addition of pockets, and in this style we would advise that a flat pocket be made with the use of a rubber band at the opening, covered with a plain flap. Many styles of pockets are made on doors, but those which take up the least possible space are desirable. As a handy provision, a robe rail may be placed at the rear of the front backs. High-grade appurtenances are used to finish the trimming, making the job complete in all details.

The amount of goods required where special colors are used for individual jobs is as follows: Three hides of leather (or its equivalent in leather substitute) for head lining, above belt line, front backs and cushions. Seven and one-half yards of cloth and about eight pounds of hair. Let the springs do the work in the cushions and backs—save other material wherever you can. Such a practice is in line with a sensible policy of conservation of resources, and is as applicable in the trim shop as anywhere else.

BRUNN / Lincoln / WEM

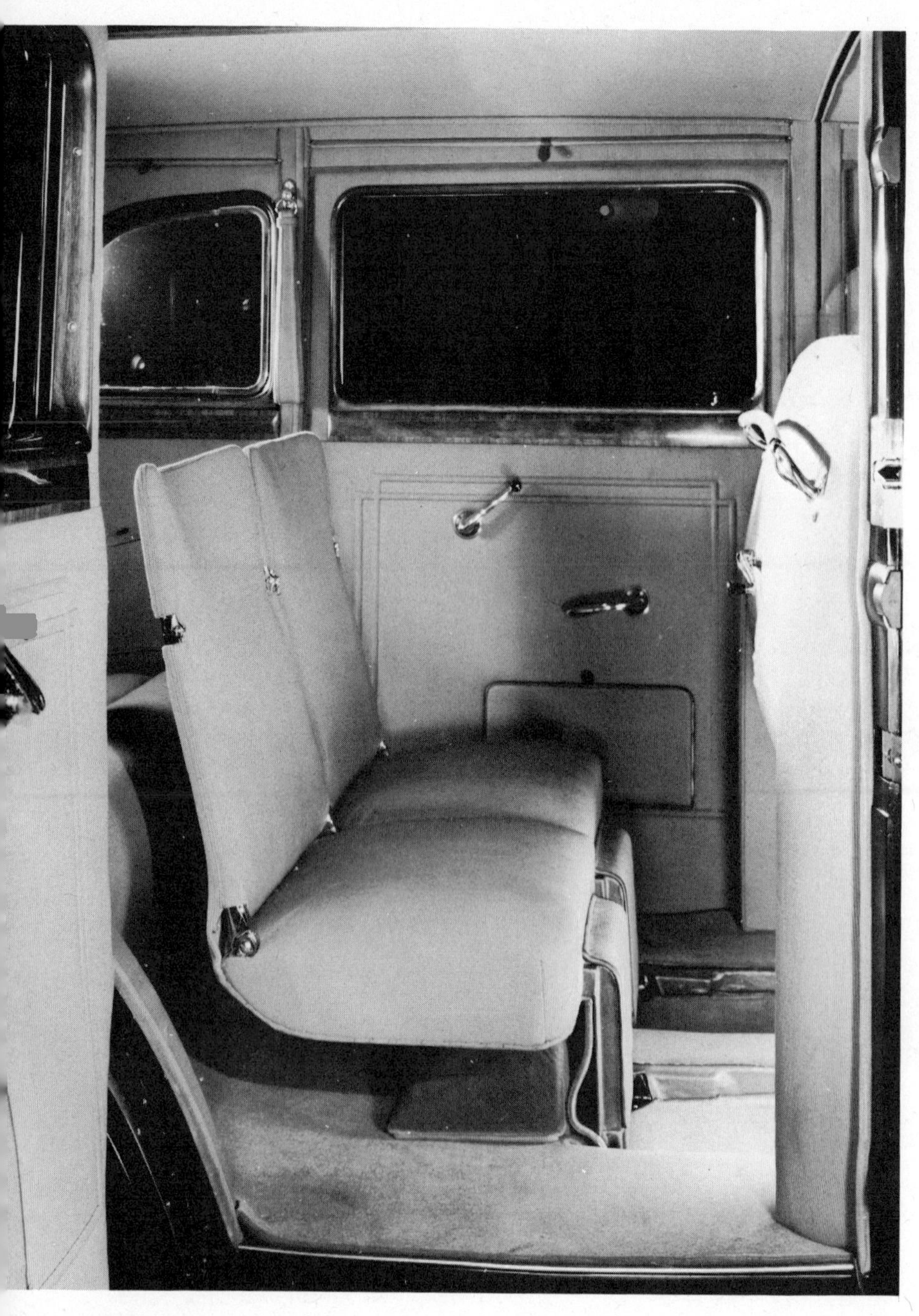

JUDKINS / Lincoln / WEM

CHAPTER XV

Fitting Up a Custom Trim Shop

No matter what subject comes up for discussion, there is always room for a difference of opinion, and so in the fitting up of the trimming department a great deal must be left to individual judgment.

How to arrange benches, fixtures, tools and stock so that everything will be handy when needed, are matters of prime importance and have a marked influence on the success or failure of the trim shop.

Practical men have frequently given useful advice on the subject of trim shop efficiency, but there is still room for improvement and suggestions that may lead to these improvements.

There is a great difference in trimming rooms, simply because different ideas prevail, but those who direct such departments should see to it that every tool and appliance is in the right place, easy to reach, without losing any valuable time.

A great deal can be learned from the factories where the wholesalers build their work, for as a rule their trimming shop is large and well ventilated, provided with sunlight or good artificial light, all the necessary appliances, and with a store-room to be proud of. But all these advantages are necessary on account of the quantity of material so rapidly handled, or everything would be in a state of chaos.

But why should not a small custom shop be run quite as economically as the large wholesale plants? The builder who employs from one to four trimmers should take care to manage his small shop as well as a large one, for in this branch of the business a larger amount of waste can be made than in any other branch, of the automobile building business.

Good Lighting Essential

The trimming room should be spacious and should be favored with abundant light and properly heated. The benches should be placed along the windows so as to obtain the best possible light and the windows should be kept clean so as not to obstruct the sun's rays. The benches should be about three feet wide and forty inches high, from the floor. The board, if composed of parts, should be well jointed, for open joints are objectionable. A large drawer for each trimmer should be under the bench, which drawer should be partitioned so as to separate the tools when placed in it, as tools should all be kept in drawers or in separate boxes.

There should be a closet large enough for the business carried on, for the storage of all trimming material, placed under lock and key, all material in order and kept so. The sewing machines should be placed in the best possible position, where good light can be had. Cover machines when not in use and be careful to keep them in good running condition, as the sewing machine is the heart of the trimming shop.

The Proper Care of Stock and Materials

There should be drawers or boxes for the enameled and patent leathers, also for ducks and rubber goods, so as to know just where to find each article when needed. Bins or barrels for hair and moss should be kept in the store-room, conveniently placed, and should be kept covered at all times.

The keeping of leathers on shelves near the ceiling should be discontinued, as the greater heat at top of room has the effect of drying out the leather, making it harsh and brittle. When in such a state and worked in a colder atmosphere it is very apt to crack and break. A chest or closet of shelves

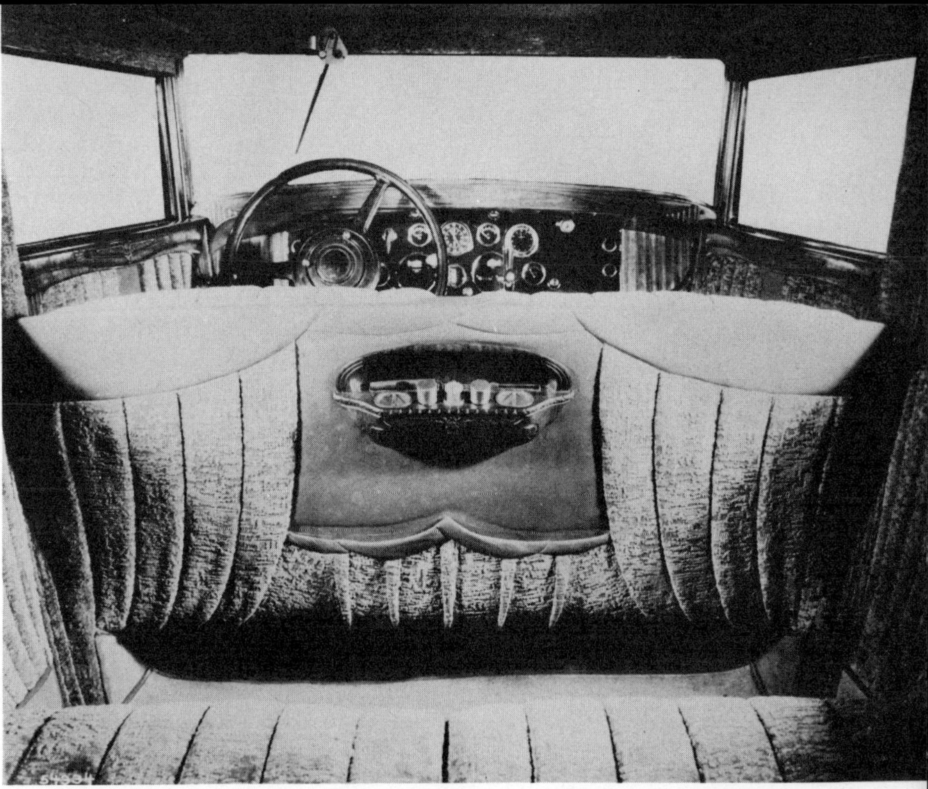

DERHAM / Duesenberg / CWM
MURPHY / Duesenberg "Beverly" / CWM

a trifle above the floor is the best place for all leather. All threads not in actual use should be kept in the box or in one of the drawers under bench, so as not to expose them to the action of sunlight, which is apt to fade the colors, or out in the atmosphere, which is apt to cause threads to decay.

"A Place for Everything"

It is also important to provide a place for every article needed by the trimmer so that dust will not settle on them, and all men employed should be requested to keep things in their proper place, thus avoiding the loss of time involved in looking for things that are not replaced. There are men so careless with their bench and tools that they are always looking for something that they have misplaced.

Another thing each man should have is a box on his bench for keeping his individual tacks, having the different kinds and sizes in this box, so that when a certain kind of tack is wanted he can see at a glance where it is. Some men have their whole bench strewn with all kinds and descriptions of tacks and can never find the one that is needed without going over the whole motley assortment. That is not efficiency.

CASTAGNA / Mercedes-Benz K / MMcC
WEYMANN / Duesenberg / CWM

WILLOUGHBY / Duesenberg / CWM
ROLLSTON / Duesenberg / CWM

CHAPTER XVI

Some Motor Car Upholstery Repairs and How to Make Them

There is always a steady demand for used cars. The appearance of the body has a great influence on the prospective customer and, in fact, its condition limits the price for which the used car will sell. Dealers are recognizing this fact and are devoting considerable time to making the body and top as presentable as possible, spending just as much as the condition of the motor, etc., will warrant, while leaving them a fair margin of profit.

Repairs to Cushions and Tops

It is often found necessary to go over the top and line it up, and many times it is the upholstery that requires attention. The cushions, particularly in the cheaper cars, always need some minor repairs. The top of the cushion is often sunken from use, even though the spring is in good condition and may need no repairs, yet the cushion must be attended to in order to give a good appearance. It can be done at a very small cost of labor.

The following method will be found to be a rapid, economical and durable cushion repair. In the cheaper grade of cushions we find that there is no wood frame at the bottom, as the facings are finished by machine in a metal tubing, so we make a wood frame the size of the spring, and attach the cushion in the condition we find it to the wood frame by means of staples. We cover the top of the cushion with a layer or two of cheap hair or substitute.

Take a piece of goods to match the trimming, which is usually a substitute leather, stretch tightly and smoothly, nail to the underneath part of the frame, turning the surplus at the corners to form a plait, blind sew the plaits, and with this simple operation we have a cushion similar to a car seat, and which often times will hold up better and have a longer life than as originally made. The backs sometimes have sunk in from use, and these repairs are as simple as the cushion, but usually requiring less labor.

Spring construction in some of the cheaper cars is often more durable than those of the higher grade cars for the

Sometimes an old cape or "one-man" top is removed on the customer's order and a neat Victoria top substituted Such a change effects quite a transformation in the appearance of the car.

reason that these springs are made the shape of the back and being made entirely of metal usually have long life; consequently we seldom have a loosened spring. So really the repairing of the back, if not torn, of course, needs only this simple treatment. The mere loosening up the top of the back, working up the hair with the rod and filling in with a small amount of hair or its substitutes, topping the back off and replacing the trimming in its original position, requires but little time and expense and adds wonderfully to the appearance. Then only a coat of dressing is required to complete the job, which pays a reasonable profit to the dealer and benefits both the purchaser and the trimmer.

New Curtain Lights Help to Sell the Used Car

When a dealer is endeavoring to dispose of a used car these minor details are the first things that attract the prospect's attention. Most of the cheaper cars use celluloid for the curtain lights, the rear curtain being the most noticeable. A vast improvement can be made in the appearance by using a window of glass with metal rim. If the size of the light used will warrant it, a new glass light can be installed without removing the rear curtain. This requires but little labor and enhances the value considerably, since the appearance is wonderfully improved and is up to date.

New Side Quarters May Be Necessary

The side quarters of the top we ofttimes find have been worn through by the saddles or bow holders. A new quarter must be made, and in order to do this quickly, we must remove the entire top, being extremely careful in chiseling out the tacks that we do not destroy the top.

It is not necessary to make a fitting of the quarter over the bows, but we remove the quarter by cutting the stitching loose at the seam line. But it should be understood that we must mark with chalk before the stitching is cut. When the quarter is removed make the fitting from the old quarter by stretching out tightly over the goods to be used; finish the quarter the same as the original, sewing it back in the old position, as marked, and replace the top in its original position. To be economical the operator must be careful not to spoil any old material, thereby making it necessary to replace with new material. This is particularly true of finishing laces.

New Carpet Improves the Appearance

Carpets in the type of work we are mentioning very often require attention. Usually on this type of work the carpets are found to be edged by machine and which sometimes frays out. It takes but a very short time to run a round binding of canvas around the rug, which is very noticeable to a purchaser making his inspection of the car's interior. If the carpet is much worn, of course it is a good investment to furnish a brand new one.

Thorough Cleaning Must Not Be Overlooked

The top should also be dressed. This helps the appearance of the car to a great extent and very materially lengthens the life of the top.

The combination lace used around the doors and backs, when worn, is unsightly, and it requires but little time to replace it. If the upholstery of the car happens to be leather or a substitute it may be easily cleaned with castile soap and lukewarm water, and in the case of leather, after being washed, it is dressed with neat's foot oil, castor oil or linseed oil, it will soften up and greatly improve in appearance and length of life.

While the above treatment of a used car, to be resold, may seem unnecessary, it has been the experience of many dealers that it is profitable when handled by an experienced mechanic, who will use his brains as well as his hands, using judgment as to how far to go in making the repairs and renovations.

Importance of Careful Estimating

In connection with the repair and overhauling of an automobile body, the person giving an estimate for such work must be extremely careful in making up his costs for doing the work. He must absolutely itemize every part of the job on which he figures, and when the job goes into the shop a copy of the items to be taken care of must accompany the car, and remain with it until the work is finished.

There is a two-fold reason for this. It is absolutely necessary that a repair card accompany the job to insure attention being given to everything figured on. This is essential in order to have satisfied customers. But it is just as necessary from the manufacturing standpoint. For in a repair job,

WILLOUGHBY / Duesenberg / CWM

when it is started through the shop, there is a great possibility of spending more for labor than was estimated on, thereby causing the manufacturer a loss. This is caused very often by doing work which was not included in the estimate and cannot be charged for. For instance, a celluloid light is found to be broken in one of the side curtains and it is repaired, yet it was not figured on in the estimate. This would entail some time to repair and would require some new material, yet there will be no return for it.

In this way many jobs in the repair shop which should have shown a fair profit have been caused to show a loss; in the greater number of cases it can be traced directly to the person making the estimate. He has been careless in itemizing the repairs to be made. The men in charge of the departments endeavor to use judgment in making repairs when no detailed, itemized card accompanies the job. But they are not mind readers and cannot be expected to know what was figured on unless it is given to them in black and white. In these times when the conservation of labor and material is of paramount importance, details of this character must be closely watched and estimates of cost strictly adhered to.

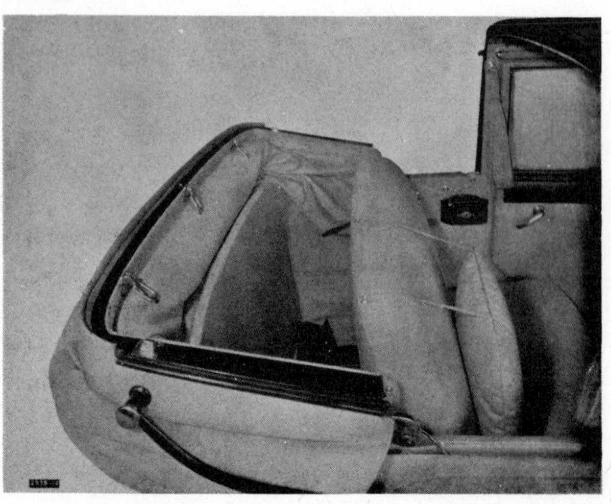

Acknowledgements

Text copy originally appeared as *Motor Car Upholstery. . A Plainly Written Book on the Fundamentals of Motor Car Trimming and Upholstery*, published by Hirst Roger, Philadelphia, 1920. Language of the original edition was reprinted exactly (even including several nebulous dull spots embroidered with dated remarks) to fully preserve for the modern restorer an unaltered perspective for authentic trimming materials and upholstering procedures. Application of these practices in restoration work will render the interiors of automobiles now revalued as the *vintage* and the *classic* at par with the original products in every important detail.

Reference to this volume was made through the Library of Vehicles.

Idea for reissue of the manual, with the addition of a showcase of supporting photographs, grew from discussions with classic trim professional Ken Sorensen, and took form with encouragement from noted illustrator and motor coachwork authority Strother MacMinn.

Coachtrim photographs were selected from private collections through the kind assistance of Charles W. Mooney, W. E. Miller, Willis B. Dobson, Jr., Strother MacMinn, William C. Kinsman and Michael McCreary.

Cover illustrations were specially drawn: the Rolls-Royce by Robert H. Gurr; the Duesenberg by Willis B. Dobson, Jr.

Index

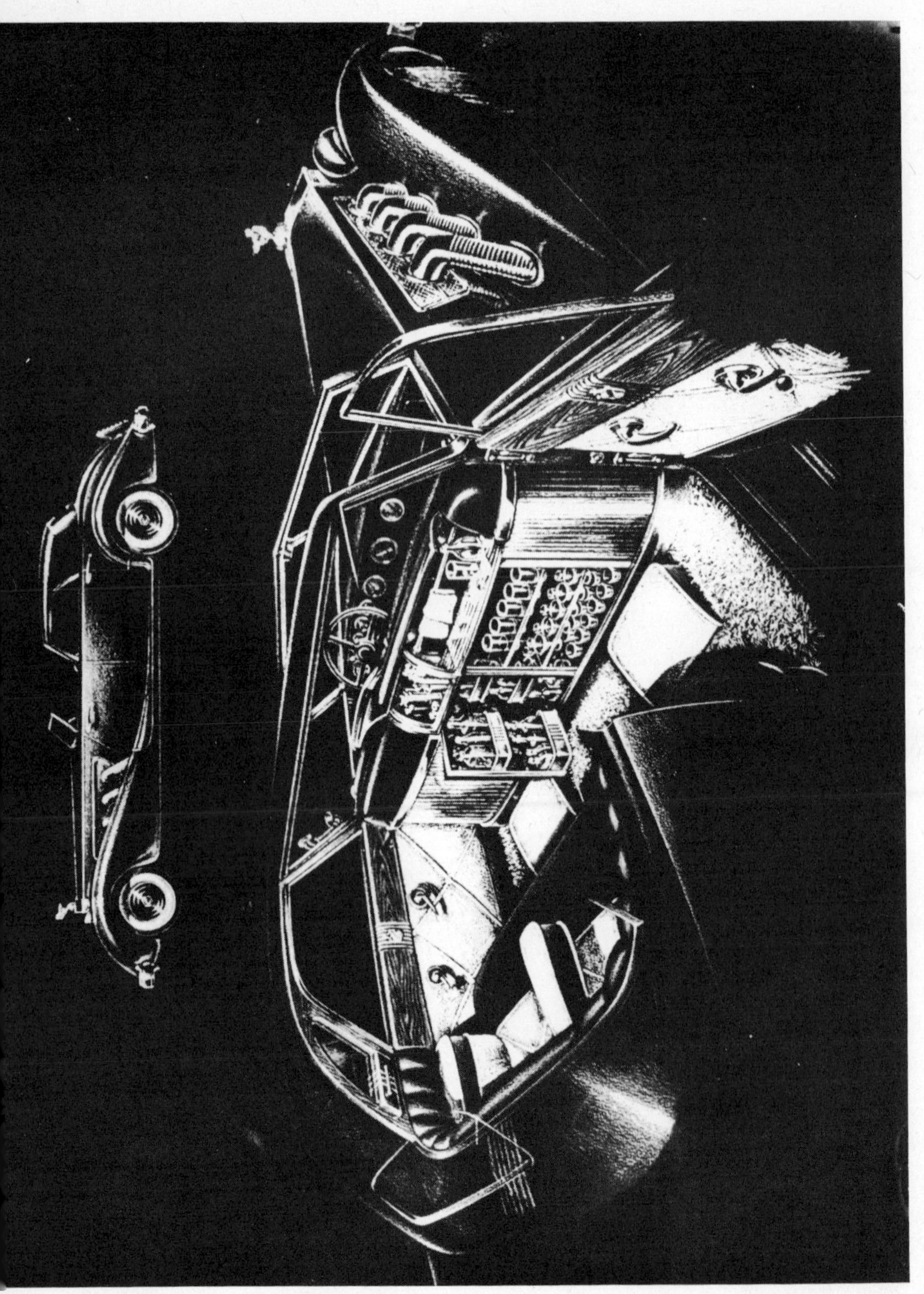

Rolls-Royce (proposed) / SMacM

LOOK FOR THE POST MARK ON MOTOR BOOKS OF SIGNIFICANCE

JESENBERG, MIGHTIEST AMERICAN OTOR CAR

ıly 480 cars were built but the Big J is legendary! Here the shoulder-straight saga of the life and times of the ɔulous classic that became a pawn in a lost era!

was a time of solid brass castings and engine-turned ıminum, of natural cowhide and quartered Circassian lnut, of hand-striped canework and whitewall tires ite on both sides. Truly it was an honest day for ɔduct. Die-castings and synthetics are ubiquitous now. neered things are for the many. Those solid things were the few.

re is a roaring saga out of the opulent Newport era— ə life and times of an elegant motor car showpiece lored for that few. Any car, deliberately designed to :ially outrank others among patricians and at the same ıe competitively outdrive (89 mph in second gear) ong playboys, would have to have been **some auto- bile.** And that, Duesenberg was!

er a generation spent in assembling one of the most ensive private automotive libraries of its kind, by 47, J. L. Elbert's spare time became overpowered by interest in the Duesenberg. Clearly, what Clark Gable n was among motion picture stars, the Duesenberg l once been among motor cars. **Once a king, always ing!** The story had never been told. . .

:h the assist of such hitherto untapped sources as ginal factory archives, correspondence was initiated h both original and then-current owners. Glowing ounts of great joy with the car came to him from ng first owners, who might reasonably have been ected to recall the car only in passive, fading memory. n Mr. Elbert launched into full scale fact-finding to her up the threads of a haughty fabric and reconstruct story from the original concept, to the present role King of the Classics. After untold hours of research came up with a penetrating account that was unique scope.

ay this book stands as the cornerstone reference for knowledgeable investigation and reporting. Startling s and sparkling anecedotes pack interest for lay ders, and carry established enthusiasts for this mar- to unchartered waters. The book is a "Duesie" and ic reading for every classic enthusiast.

illustrations / 168 pages (8½ x 11") indexed. Hard- nd, silver-stamped, $8. postpaid

ROLLS-ROYCE, THE LIVING LEGEND

Certain to become a collector's item in years to come this volume stands unchallenged as the veritable fountainhead of antique and vintage Rolls lore!

The tale of a grandeur reflected from ageless technical excellence is told through the faithful reproduction of half a century of contemporary Company-issued British and American sales and institutional literature. No less than 25 catalogs and special brochures are featured, along with other items representing nearly 500 pages from original authorized factory printings. Over 350 photographs and line illustrations portray the compelling construction finesse, mechanical innovation and coachwork which brought timbre to **The Name.**

Two earlier volumes THE AMERICAN ROLLS (1951) and THE BRITISH ROLLS (1953), both now long out-of-print, were widely acclaimed as unparalleled reference sources. The present volume under the new title combines all the original matter from both of these books in an expanded, indexed format.

350 illustrations / 384 pages (6 x 9") indexed. Hardbound, gold-stamped, $10. postpaid

ORDER TODAY
FOR YOUR PLEASURE TOMORROW!

WHEN YOU ORDER DIRECTLY from Post Motor Books, the publishers, you can depend on FAST HANDLING of your order with same-day postpaid shipment in protective cartons—with COMPLETE SATISFACTION guaranteed or money back.

CALIFORNIA orders please include 5% sales tax. C.O.D. orders are not encouraged (on account of extra bother and expense to you) but will be processed on your specific request (domestic only). FOREIGN orders please add 5% to book prices to meet special wrapping requirements and postage; please remit in U.S. funds only. ORDER TODAY for your pleasure tomorrow!

'ou may receive IMMEDIATE SHIPMENT by remitting directly to the publisher:
Post Motor Books / Box 150 / Arcadia, California 91006

The Vintage Craft Series

Uniform binding / $4 each / postpaid from the publisher

Each volume, written and illustrated in graphic detail by recognized contemporary authorities of that golden era before the Wars, revives one of the motor body hand crafts in full, comprehensive dimension—out of the limbo where it was buried under the avalanche of automatic machines that swept body building practice generally after World War I.

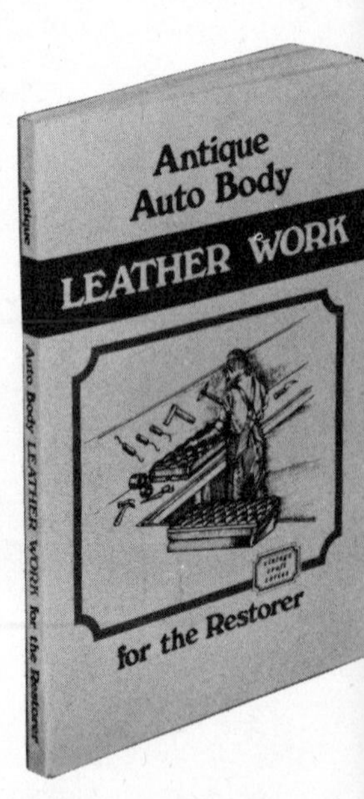

VALUABLE REFERENCE FOR EVERY OLD CAR ENTHUSIAST—AND AS HELPFUL AS BLUEPRINTS FOR THE SERIOUS RESTORER!

METAL WORK/Authentic sheet metal layout for steel and aluminum

The geometric procedure for developing patterns required for every body panel unfold with the support of 150 line illustrations, including many scale demonstration layouts with various optional treatments for hoods, cowls, seats, doors, fenders, aprons, complete bodies, etc.

WOOD WORK/Authentic framing and paneling practice

Every facet from selection and measurement of material and body drafting for structure and rigidity, through shaping, joints used, finishing, paneling work, iron fittings, door hanging, etc. detailed with 180 supporting line illustrations, including demonstration layouts with various options for a number of open and closed body styles.

LEATHER WORK/Authentic leather trimming practice

Thorough coverage in exacting detail, from selection o material to layout of diamond tufting, determining full ness, pleating, buttoning, paneling and finishing, a well as procedures with fabrics and lace for closed bod types, is backed up with a profusion of line drawings an diagrams, including typical layouts for various body types

TOP WORK/Authentic touring car top construction practice

Complete procedure for determining proper dimension and placement of top bows from given body measure ments, designing, layout and fabrication of the cape typ (multi-bowed collapsible) top with details for straps pads, storm fronts, side curtains, back curtains, etc supported lavishly with illustrations.

UNIFORM 6″ x 9″ LEATHERETTE/$4 each/postpaid fro the publisher.

You may receive IMMEDIATE SHIPMENT by remitting directly to the publisher
Post Motor Books / Box 150 / Arcadia, California 91006